Harmony and Temptation: A Journey Through the History of The Temptations.

By D. Wayne Moore

Chapter 1: The Origins of Motown: The Birth of a Musical Movement.

In the early 1960s, a cultural revolution was brewing in the heart of Detroit, Michigan. It was a time of social and political change, but amidst the tumult, a unique musical movement began to emerge. This movement, which would later become known as Motown, would reshape the landscape of popular music and leave an indelible mark on the world.

The origins of Motown can be traced back to a young man named Berry Gordy Jr. Born on November 28, 1929, in Detroit, Gordy had a passion for music from an early age. He was inspired by the vibrant sounds of rhythm and blues, jazz, and gospel that filled the streets of his city. Gordy harbored dreams of creating a record label that would produce music that transcended racial and cultural boundaries.

Motown's story began to take shape in 1959 when Gordy founded Tamla Records, which would eventually evolve into Motown Records. He set up a modest studio in a small house on West Grand Boulevard, which would become the legendary Hitsville USA. Armed with determination and an unwavering vision, Gordy sought to create a distinctive sound that would appeal to a wide audience.

One of Gordy's guiding principles was to develop and groom talented artists. He wanted to provide opportunities for African American artists who were often overlooked by major record labels at the time. With an eye for talent and an emphasis on professionalism, Gordy assembled a roster of incredible artists, including Smokey Robinson, Diana Ross and the Supremes, Stevie Wonder, Marvin Gaye, and the Temptations, among others.

Motown's sound was a fusion of various musical genres, incorporating elements of rhythm and blues, pop, soul, and funk. The label's in-house songwriting and production team, known as "The Funk Brothers," created catchy melodies and infectious rhythms that resonated with audiences. The Motown sound was characterized by its polished and sophisticated arrangements, silky harmonies, and infectious grooves.

Gordy also understood the importance of presentation and marketing. He implemented rigorous artist development programs, grooming his artists not only as musicians but also as performers. The Motown artists were known for their impeccable style, choreographed dance moves, and charismatic stage presence. Gordy aimed to create a complete entertainment package that would captivate audiences both musically and visually.

Motown quickly gained traction and achieved widespread success. The label released a string of chart-topping hits that dominated the airwaves and captured the hearts of millions. Songs like "My Girl" by the Temptations, "Shop Around" by the Miracles, and "Dancing in the Street" by Martha and the Vandellas became anthems of a generation.

Motown's impact extended far beyond the music industry. It played a crucial role in breaking down racial barriers in popular culture. The label's success demonstrated that music could be a unifying force, transcending divisions of race and ethnicity. Motown's artists became household names and served as cultural ambassadors, spreading joy and inspiring countless individuals around the world.

The birth of Motown was a testament to the indomitable spirit of Berry Gordy Jr. and the artists who believed in his vision. Against all odds, they created a musical movement that would forever change the course of popular music. Motown's legacy continues to resonate today, reminding us of the power of music to bring people together and create positive change.

As the 1960s gave way to the 1970s, Motown faced new challenges and underwent transformations. However, the impact of its early years remains a testament to the enduring power of the Motown sound. The origins of Motown and the birth of this musical movement set the stage for a revolution in popular music, leaving an indelible mark on the industry and inspiring generations to come.

Chapter 2: Detroit in the 1950s: The Rich Cultural Landscape

In the 1950s, the city of Detroit, Michigan, pulsated with a vibrant cultural energy that permeated every aspect of its society. Known as the Motor City for its booming automobile industry, Detroit was also a hotbed of cultural diversity and artistic expression. During this transformative decade, the city became a melting pot of ideas, music, and creativity, shaping the cultural landscape in profound ways.

At the heart of Detroit's cultural landscape in the 1950s was its African American community. The Great Migration, a mass movement of African Americans from the rural South to northern cities, brought a wave of new residents to Detroit. This influx of talent, energy, and aspirations enriched the city's cultural fabric, contributing to the emergence of vibrant neighborhoods like Black Bottom and Paradise Valley.

Black Bottom, located on Detroit's east side, became a thriving center of African American life and culture. It was a bustling neighborhood filled with jazz clubs, theaters, and businesses owned by African Americans. The Paradise Theatre, a renowned entertainment venue, attracted legendary performers such as Duke Ellington, Ella Fitzgerald, and Count Basie. The vibrant nightlife and artistic community in Black Bottom fostered an atmosphere of creativity and innovation.

Music played a pivotal role in shaping the cultural landscape of Detroit in the 1950s. Jazz, rhythm and blues, gospel, and early forms of rock and roll reverberated through the city's clubs and theaters. Detroit's own Motown Records, founded in 1959, would later emerge as a global phenomenon, but its roots were firmly planted in the rich musical traditions of the city. Artists like John Lee Hooker, Aretha Franklin, and Jackie Wilson honed their craft in the Detroit music scene, laying the foundation for the Motown sound that would captivate the world. Beyond music, Detroit in the 1950s was a hub for visual arts and literature. The Detroit Artists Market, established in 1932, provided a platform for local artists to showcase their work. The Detroit Institute of Arts, with its extensive collection of renowned masterpieces, inspired and nurtured a new generation of artists. The city's vibrant art community fostered creativity and encouraged artists to push boundaries and explore new forms of expression.

Literature also thrived in Detroit during this era. Poets, writers, and intellectuals congregated in coffeehouses and literary salons, engaging in intellectual discussions and sharing their literary works. Writers like Gwendolyn Brooks, who became the first African American to win the Pulitzer Prize for Poetry in 1950, contributed to Detroit's literary legacy.

In addition to its cultural contributions, Detroit in the 1950s was also a crucible for social and political change. The city was a center of the civil rights movement, as activists fought against racial segregation and inequality. Organizations like the National Association for the Advancement of Colored People (NAACP) and the Congress of Racial Equality (CORE) spearheaded efforts to challenge discriminatory practices and promote equal rights for all.

The cultural landscape of 1950s Detroit was a reflection of the city's resilience, creativity, and diversity. It was a time when artists, musicians, and intellectuals converged, creating a fertile ground for innovation and expression. The vibrant neighborhoods, the pulsating music scene, the flourishing arts community, and the push for social change all combined to make Detroit a cultural powerhouse.

However, the 1950s also laid the groundwork for significant challenges that the city would face in the decades to come. Economic shifts, racial tensions, and urban decay would later shape a different narrative for Detroit. Nevertheless, the cultural legacy forged in the 1950s remains a testament to the enduring spirit of Detroit and its contribution to American culture as a whole.

Chapter 3: Forming the Foundations: Early Years of The Temptations.

The Temptations, one of the most influential and iconic vocal groups in the history of popular music, had humble beginnings that laid the foundation for their legendary career. Emerging from the streets of Detroit in the early 1960s, The Temptations would go on to captivate audiences with their impeccable harmonies, polished choreography, and soulful performances. This chapter explores the early years of The Temptations, tracing their journey from their formation to their rise as Motown superstars. The story of The Temptations begins in the neighborhoods of Detroit, where a group of talented young singers with a shared love for music came together. Eddie Kendricks, Paul Williams, Otis

Williams, Melvin Franklin, and Elbridge "Al" Bryant formed the original lineup of the group, known as The Elgins. They began singing together in local talent shows, honing their vocal skills and captivating audiences with their harmonies.

In 1961, The Elgins caught the attention of Berry Gordy Jr., the founder of Motown Records. Impressed by their talent and potential, Gordy signed them to the label, and they changed their name to The Temptations. The group's lineup underwent some changes during this time, with Al Bryant being replaced by David Ruffin, who would become one of the most iconic lead vocalists in the history of the group.

Under the guidance of Motown's meticulous artist development programs, The Temptations refined their skills and developed their signature sound. They worked closely with Motown's talented songwriting and production team, including Smokey Robinson, Norman Whitfield, and Holland-Dozier-Holland, who crafted hits tailor-made for the group. The collaboration between The Temptations and these talented songwriters would prove to be a winning formula. The Temptations' early recordings showcased their versatility, blending elements of doo-wop, rhythm and blues, and soul. Songs like "The Way You Do the Things You Do" and "My Girl" became instant classics, capturing the hearts of audiences across the nation. With David Ruffin's passionate and emotive lead vocals, backed by the seamless harmonies of the group, The Temptations carved a distinct sound that resonated with listeners.

Beyond their musical prowess, The Temptations were known for their impeccable style and choreography. With their sharp suits, synchronized dance moves, and charismatic stage presence, they set a new standard for showmanship. Their performances became spectacles, captivating audiences and setting the stage for their reputation as consummate entertainers.

However, behind the scenes, The Temptations faced their share of challenges. Internal tensions, personal struggles, and the pressures of fame threatened to derail the group. Paul Williams, one of the founding members, battled personal demons and health issues, eventually leading to his departure from the group. Despite these challenges, The Temptations persevered, driven by their love for music and their determination to succeed.

As the 1960s progressed, The Temptations' success continued to soar. They released a string of hits that topped the charts, including "Ain't Too

Proud to Beg," "I Can't Get Next to You," and "Papa Was a Rollin' Stone." These songs showcased the group's evolution, incorporating elements of funk and psychedelic soul while retaining their distinctive harmonies.

The Temptations' influence extended far beyond their chart success. They became role models for aspiring artists, breaking down racial barriers and paving the way for future generations of African American musicians. Their music was a soundtrack to the civil rights movement, providing a voice of hope, resilience, and empowerment.

The early years of The Temptations set the stage for their enduring legacy. Their harmonies, showmanship, and timeless hits continue to captivate audiences today. The group's ability to evolve and adapt to changing musical landscapes while staying true to their roots is a testament to their artistry and creativity. The Temptations' journey from the streets of Detroit to international stardom is a testament to the power of music and the resilience of the human spirit.

Chapter 4: The Primes: Predecessors of The Temptations

Before The Temptations emerged as the iconic vocal group we know today, there was a predecessor group that laid the groundwork for their success. The Primes, a talented quartet from Detroit, served as a stepping stone for the formation of The Temptations, showcasing their harmonies, stage presence, and immense potential. This chapter delves into the early years of The Primes, exploring their journey and their significant impact on the formation of The Temptations.

The Primes were formed in the late 1950s and consisted of four members: Eddie Kendricks, Paul Williams, Kell Osborne, and Wiley Waller. They honed their vocal skills through local performances and quickly gained a reputation for their tight harmonies and polished performances. Drawing inspiration from doo-wop and rhythm and blues, The Primes began making waves in the vibrant Detroit music scene.

Although The Primes never achieved the commercial success that would later come to The Temptations, their talent and artistry set the stage for the group's future endeavors. Their performances in local venues and talent shows caught the attention of Berry Gordy Jr., the founder of Motown Records. Impressed by their abilities, Gordy signed The Primes to the label in 1960, marking their entry into the Motown family.

While signed to Motown, The Primes released several singles, including "Thinking About My Baby" and "The Miracle," showcasing their harmonies and the soulful lead vocals of Eddie Kendricks. These recordings showcased their potential, but they failed to make a significant impact on the charts. Despite this, their time at Motown allowed them to form relationships with key figures within the label and further develop their musical abilities.

The Primes' tenure at Motown was short-lived, and internal conflicts led to their disbandment. However, the group's dissolution would ultimately pave the way for the formation of a new vocal powerhouse: The Temptations. Eddie Kendricks and Paul Williams, two of the founding members of The Primes, would go on to become integral parts of

The Temptations' lineup, leaving an indelible mark on the group's sound and success.

Eddie Kendricks, with his distinctive falsetto, would become one of The Temptations' lead vocalists, infusing their music with a captivating and soulful quality. Paul Williams brought his powerful and emotive voice to the group, contributing to their signature sound. Their experiences and musical chemistry from their time as The Primes would carry over seamlessly into The Temptations.

The Primes' influence on The Temptations extended beyond their musical contributions. Their experiences as a struggling group navigating the challenges of the music industry would shape the resilience and determination of The Temptations. The lessons learned during their time as The Primes would prove invaluable as they faced the trials and tribulations of building a successful career.

The Primes may not have achieved the same level of recognition as The Temptations, but their contributions cannot be underestimated. They laid the groundwork for the harmonies, showmanship, and vocal prowess that would become hallmarks of The Temptations' success. The experiences and musical foundation established by The Primes were vital in shaping the group's trajectory and their eventual status as Motown superstars.

In the grand narrative of The Temptations, The Primes serve as a crucial chapter, showcasing the early years of the group's key members and the formation of their unique sound. The Primes' legacy lives on as a testament to the talent and determination that would ultimately propel The Temptations to become one of the most beloved and influential vocal groups in the history of popular music.

Chapter 5: The Distants: Forming the Core of the Future Group

Before The Temptations solidified their lineup and rose to stardom, another group played a pivotal role in shaping their foundation. The Distants, a talented vocal group from Detroit, formed the core of what would later become The Temptations. This chapter explores the early years of The Distants, their musical journey, and their significant impact on the formation and direction of The Temptations.

The Distants were originally formed in the late 1950s and consisted of three members: Otis Williams, Elbridge "Al" Bryant, and Melvin Franklin. These three talented vocalists came together with a shared passion for music and a desire to make their mark in the industry. Drawing inspiration from doo-wop and rhythm and blues, The Distants began honing their harmonies and vocal skills. During their early years, The Distants performed at local venues, talent shows, and street corners, showcasing their talents to anyone who would listen. Their smooth harmonies and soulful delivery captured the attention of Berry Gordy Jr., the founder of Motown Records. Recognizing their potential, Gordy signed The Distants to Motown in 1959, marking the beginning of their association with the label.

The Distants released several singles during their time at Motown, including "Come On" and "Come On" (Reprise). These recordings showcased their vocal prowess and hinted at the promise of greater success. However, despite their talents, The Distants struggled to achieve significant commercial success, and internal tensions eventually led to changes within the group. While The Distants didn't achieve the level of recognition they had hoped for, their impact on The Temptations cannot be overstated. Otis Williams, the founding member of The Distants, would go on to become a key figure in the formation and longevity of The Temptations. His vision, leadership, and commitment to the group's success would prove instrumental in shaping their trajectory. With the addition of Eddie Kendricks, Paul Williams, and later David Ruffin, The Temptations began to take shape, drawing from the talents and experiences of both The Primes and The Distants. The core members of The Distants provided the foundation for The Temptations' harmonies, with Otis Williams anchoring the group's lineup as its only remaining original member.

The Distants' influence on The Temptations extended beyond their vocal abilities. Their experiences navigating the music industry, the challenges they faced, and the lessons learned along the way contributed to the resilience and determination of The Temptations. The merging of talents from The Distants and The Primes created a dynamic and versatile vocal group that would go on to captivate audiences worldwide.

The story of The Distants serves as a testament to the power of perseverance and the importance of collaboration. Although they did not achieve significant commercial success themselves, their impact as a core component of The Temptations is undeniable. Their contributions helped shape the group's sound, style, and legacy, setting the stage for The Temptations' eventual rise to superstardom.

As The Temptations' journey continued, The Distants' legacy lived on, reminding them of their roots and the collective experiences that brought them together. The merging of talents from The Distants, The Primes, and additional members formed a harmonious union that would stand the test of time and solidify The Temptations as one of the greatest vocal groups in the history of popular music.

The Distants may have been a group that faded into the background, but their impact on The Temptations' success and enduring legacy remains imprinted in the annals of music history. Their story serves as a testament to the transformative power of collaboration, talent, and perseverance, forever woven into the fabric of The Temptations' remarkable journey.

Chapter 6: The Temptations' Formation and Early Struggles

The Temptations, renowned as one of the most iconic vocal groups of all time, had a humble and challenging beginning that tested their resolve and determination. This chapter delves into the formation of The Temptations and explores the early struggles they faced as they embarked on their journey to success.

With the merging of talents from The Primes and The Distants, The Temptations began to take shape in the early 1960s. The group's lineup included Eddie Kendricks, Paul Williams, Otis Williams, Melvin Franklin, and Elbridge "Al" Bryant, with Otis Williams serving as the sole remaining original member from The Distants. Their diverse musical backgrounds and exceptional vocal abilities set the stage for something extraordinary.

The formation of The Temptations coincided with their signing to Motown Records, under the guidance of Berry Gordy Jr. Gordy recognized the potential of the group and saw the opportunity to mold them into something special. However, the early years were not without their struggles. The Temptations faced numerous obstacles, both internally and externally, that tested their unity and commitment to their musical aspirations.

One of the significant challenges The Temptations encountered was navigating the competitive and cutthroat nature of the music industry. Motown Records, while a powerhouse of talent, also had a roster of formidable artists vying for success. The group had to work tirelessly to stand out among their labelmates and capture the attention of both the industry and audiences.

Furthermore, The Temptations faced personal and professional conflicts within the group. Elbridge "Al" Bryant, one of the original members, struggled with alcoholism and exhibited unreliability. These challenges strained the cohesion of the group and led to Bryant's departure, making way for the addition of David Ruffin in 1964. Ruffin's charismatic presence and powerful vocals would soon become a defining element of The Temptations' sound.

Despite the internal struggles, The Temptations also faced external difficulties in gaining recognition and achieving commercial success. Their early releases, while showcasing their immense talent, failed to make a significant impact on the charts. They were still searching for their distinctive sound and a breakthrough hit that would propel them to stardom.

The turning point for The Temptations came in 1964 when Smokey Robinson penned the timeless classic, "The Way You Do the Things You Do." The song, released as a single, became their first major hit, reaching the Top 20 on the Billboard charts. It not only showcased their harmonies but also introduced audiences to the charismatic and emotive lead vocals of David Ruffin, solidifying his place as the group's frontman.

With their breakthrough hit, The Temptations gained momentum and began to solidify their unique sound and style. They teamed up with songwriters and producers like Norman Whitfield and Holland-Dozier-Holland, who crafted hits that fused soul, R&B, and pop sensibilities. Songs like "My Girl," "Ain't Too Proud to Beg," and "Get

Ready" further cemented their status as hitmakers and propelled them into the forefront of popular music.

While their chart success grew, The Temptations continued to face personal and professional challenges. The group's demanding touring schedule and the temptations of fame put a strain on their relationships and personal lives. Paul Williams, in particular, battled health issues and struggled with depression, leading to his eventual departure from the group.

Through perseverance and the unwavering commitment to their craft, The Temptations overcame their early struggles and emerged as true superstars. Their smooth harmonies, polished choreography, and electrifying stage presence captivated audiences worldwide. The group's ability to seamlessly blend soul, pop, and R&B, coupled with their captivating performances, set them apart from their contemporaries.

The Temptations' formation and early struggles were a crucible that forged their resilience, determination, and unwavering pursuit of musical excellence. Their journey serves as a testament to the power of perseverance, unity, and the transformative nature of music. From their modest beginnings to their rise as cultural icons, The Temptations' legacy continues to inspire and resonate with audiences, solidifying their place in music history.

Chapter 7: The Transition: Merging The Primes and The Distants

As The Temptations navigated their early struggles and searched for their distinctive sound, a significant transition occurred that would shape the group's trajectory. The merging of The Primes and The Distants brought together a wealth of talent, harmonies, and experiences, solidifying The Temptations' identity and paving the way for their future success. This chapter explores the transition period and the transformative impact of combining these two influential vocal groups.

The merging of The Primes and The Distants was not a seamless process. It required a delicate balance of personalities, artistic visions, and the shared goal of creating something extraordinary. Eddie Kendricks and Paul Williams from The Primes joined forces with Otis Williams, Melvin Franklin, and Elbridge "Al" Bryant from The Distants, forming a powerful vocal quintet.

Each member brought their unique vocal stylings and personalities to the table, resulting in a harmonious blend of talents. Eddie Kendricks' soulful falsetto and Paul Williams' dynamic voice added depth and dimension to the group's sound. Otis Williams provided stability and leadership as the sole original member from The Distants, while Melvin Franklin's rich bass vocals added a captivating foundation to their harmonies. Elbridge "Al" Bryant, though short-lived in his tenure, contributed to the group's early development. During this transition period, The Temptations were refining their musical style and searching for the sound that would set them apart. The influences of doo-wop, rhythm and blues, and the emerging Motown sound were melded together, creating a distinct and innovative sound that would become synonymous with The Temptations.

As The Temptations solidified their lineup, they began honing their stage presence and choreography. Drawing inspiration from the Motown family, they developed synchronized dance routines that would become an integral part of their performances, captivating audiences with their polished and energetic showmanship.

The merging of The Primes and The Distants brought not only vocal prowess but also a shared history of perseverance and determination. Both groups had experienced their fair share of struggles and setbacks, and the merging of their talents symbolized a collective drive to overcome obstacles and succeed in the music industry.

This period of transition was not without its challenges. The group faced internal conflicts and tensions as they adjusted to the dynamics of their new lineup. The departure of Elbridge "Al" Bryant due to personal issues led to the addition of David Ruffin, who would go on to become an integral part of The Temptations' success. Ruffin's charismatic stage presence and soulful vocals added a new dimension to the group's sound, further elevating their artistry.

With the amalgamation of talents from The Primes and The Distants, The Temptations began to carve out their own identity within the Motown family. The distinctive harmonies, dynamic lead vocals, and captivating stage performances set them apart from their peers, and their evolution as a group gained traction.

The merging of The Primes and The Distants laid the foundation for The Temptations' future endeavors. Their experiences, influences, and collective determination shaped the group's trajectory, forging a path to success that would transcend time and resonate with audiences across generations.

As The Temptations embarked on their journey, the transition period proved to be a pivotal moment in their history. The merging of talents, the development of their signature sound, and the strengthening of their unity propelled them towards becoming one of the most influential and beloved vocal groups in music history.

The Temptations' transition represented the culmination of perseverance, collaboration, and artistic exploration. It marked the beginning of a new chapter for the group, as they embraced their collective identity and embarked on a path that would lead them to global recognition and musical immortality.

Chapter 8: The Name Change: Becoming The Temptations

In their quest for musical success and a unique identity, The Temptations faced a pivotal moment that would forever shape their trajectory—the decision to change their name. This chapter delves into the reasons behind the name change and the significance it held in solidifying their artistic direction and legacy.

Originally known as The Elgins, the group encountered legal issues with another artist using a similar name. This predicament prompted a search for a new name that would capture their essence and resonate with audiences. After much consideration, The Temptations emerged as the moniker that would come to define the group's extraordinary journey.

The name "The Temptations" embodied the magnetic allure of their performances and the seductive quality of their music. It reflected their ability to captivate audiences and evoke a range of emotions through their soulful harmonies and electrifying stage presence. The name change signaled a shift in their artistic direction and a commitment to creating music that would tempt and mesmerize listeners.

With their new name in place, The Temptations sought to redefine themselves and make a lasting impact in the music industry. They honed their sound, further refining their harmonies, and delved into recording sessions that would produce hits that transcended genre boundaries.

The significance of the name change went beyond its marketing appeal. It represented a newfound confidence and maturity within the group. The

Temptations understood that they were not just performers, but artists who were determined to push boundaries, challenge societal norms, and deliver music that resonated with the human experience.

Under the guidance of Motown Records and the creative vision of producers and songwriters like Smokey Robinson, Norman Whitfield, and Holland-Dozier-Holland, The Temptations began to create a distinct sound that blended elements of soul, R&B, and pop. Their music became a powerful force that not only entertained but also conveyed messages of love, social consciousness, and resilience.

Hits like "My Girl," "Papa Was a Rollin' Stone," and "Ain't Too Proud to Beg" showcased The Temptations' versatility and their ability to deliver both heartfelt ballads and energetic, socially-charged anthems. Their music resonated with audiences of all backgrounds, transcending racial and cultural barriers and solidifying their place in music history.

The name change to The Temptations marked a turning point in the group's career, setting the stage for their ascent to superstardom. It became a brand that represented excellence, innovation, and artistic integrity. The group's dedication to their craft, their commitment to pushing musical boundaries, and their ability to connect with audiences on a profound level were all embodied in their new identity.

Beyond the name itself, The Temptations' success hinged on the collective talents and contributions of its members—Eddie Kendricks, Paul Williams, Otis Williams, Melvin Franklin, and David Ruffin. Each member brought their unique voice, style, and charisma to the group, creating a dynamic blend of individual talents that became the hallmark of The Temptations' sound.

The name change to The Temptations was a symbolic transformation that represented the group's artistic evolution and the culmination of their collective journey. It encapsulated their ability to tempt and enchant listeners with their music, leaving an indelible mark on popular culture.

As The Temptations continued to evolve and leave an indelible mark on the music industry, their name change served as a reminder of their unwavering commitment to their artistry. It became synonymous with excellence, creativity, and the enduring legacy of a group that dared to challenge conventions and redefine the boundaries of popular music.

The name change to The Temptations was a defining moment that propelled the group towards unrivaled success and established their rightful place as one of the greatest vocal groups of all time.

Chapter 9: Finding Their Voice: Early Musical Direction and Influences.

As The Temptations embarked on their musical journey, they embarked on a quest to find their unique voice and artistic direction. This chapter explores the group's early influences and the evolution of their musical style, highlighting the factors that shaped their sound and set them apart from their contemporaries.

The Temptations drew inspiration from a rich tapestry of musical genres, blending elements of soul, R&B, gospel, and pop to create a sound that was uniquely their own. Their early influences can be traced back to the gospel roots of their upbringing, which instilled in them a deep appreciation for rich vocal harmonies and heartfelt expressions of faith.

Growing up in church choirs, The Temptations honed their vocal abilities, learning to blend their voices in harmonious unison. This early training laid the foundation for the seamless harmonies that would become their trademark. They infused their music with the spirit and emotion of gospel, bringing a soulful and transcendent quality to their performances.

The Motown sound, with its infectious melodies and polished production, also played a significant role in shaping The Temptations' musical direction. As part of the Motown family, they were influenced by labelmates such as The Supremes, The Four Tops, and Stevie Wonder. Motown's signature style blended pop sensibilities with R&B and soul, and The Temptations embraced this approach, incorporating catchy hooks, smooth melodies, and tight vocal arrangements into their own repertoire.

The creative collaborations between The Temptations and Motown's talented songwriters and producers were instrumental in defining their sound. Artists like Smokey Robinson, Holland-Dozier-Holland, and Norman Whitfield crafted songs that perfectly complemented the group's vocal abilities and allowed them to showcase their range and versatility. From the infectious pop-soul of "Get Ready" to the socially conscious epic "Papa Was a Rollin' Stone," these collaborations propelled The Temptations to new heights of artistic expression.

Beyond the Motown influences, The Temptations drew inspiration from a diverse array of musical sources. They admired and incorporated elements of the vocal harmonies of doo-wop groups, the rhythmic drive of early rock and roll, and the emotional depth of the blues. By weaving these influences together, The Temptations created a sound that resonated with audiences of all backgrounds, transcending genres and becoming a musical force in their own right.

One of the defining features of The Temptations' early musical direction was their ability to seamlessly blend lead vocals and harmonies. They employed a rotating lead vocalist approach, with David Ruffin, Eddie Kendricks, and later Dennis Edwards, each taking turns at the forefront. This dynamic allowed for a variety of vocal textures and personalities to shine through, contributing to the group's captivating performances and distinct sound.

Another aspect that set The Temptations apart was their commitment to delivering meaningful and socially conscious messages through their music. In an era marked by civil rights struggles and social unrest, The Temptations used their platform to address issues of love, inequality, and the human experience. Their songs carried depth and significance, resonating with listeners on a personal and universal level.

The Temptations' ability to find their voice and craft a sound that was uniquely theirs was a testament to their artistic vision and their dedication to their craft. Their early influences, combined with their collaborative spirit and the innovative approach of Motown, allowed them to transcend musical boundaries and leave an indelible mark on popular culture.

As The Temptations continued to evolve, their sound became synonymous with soulful harmonies, infectious melodies, and a social consciousness that mirrored the changing times. Their ability to fuse diverse musical influences into a cohesive and compelling whole solidified their place as icons of the music industry.

In finding their voice, The Temptations carved out a musical legacy that would endure for generations. Their early influences and the unique blend of styles and genres that defined their sound cemented their status as one of the greatest vocal groups of all time. The Temptations had not only found their voice but had discovered a musical language that spoke to the hearts and souls of millions around the world.

Chapter 10: David Ruffin: The New Lead Singer

With the departure of Elbridge "Al" Bryant, The Temptations found themselves in search of a new lead singer to complement their evolving sound. It was during this period that David Ruffin entered the scene, bringing with him a mesmerizing voice and an unforgettable stage presence. This chapter delves into David Ruffin's arrival and his impact as the new lead singer of The Temptations.

David Ruffin's journey to joining The Temptations was not an easy one. Born on January 18, 1941, in Whynot, Mississippi, Ruffin developed a passion for music at a young age. His powerful and soulful voice set him apart, catching the attention of record producers and eventually leading him to Detroit, the epicenter of the Motown sound.

In 1964, Ruffin auditioned for Berry Gordy, the founder of Motown Records, and his voice immediately captivated the room. Recognizing Ruffin's immense talent, Gordy introduced him to The Temptations, who were searching for a new lead singer. The chemistry was instantaneous, and it became clear that Ruffin's voice and magnetic stage presence would take the group to new heights.

Ruffin's voice possessed a raw and emotional quality that perfectly complemented the harmonies of The Temptations. His distinctive tenor had a gritty edge, filled with passion and vulnerability. Whether he was belting out a powerful ballad or delivering a soulful and tender performance, Ruffin's vocals left an indelible mark on the group's sound.

One of the most iconic moments of Ruffin's tenure with The Temptations was his lead vocal on the timeless classic "My Girl." Released in 1964, the song became an instant hit and solidified The Temptations' status as superstars. Ruffin's rich and velvety voice carried the song's heartfelt lyrics with sincerity and charm, captivating listeners around the world. "My Girl" remains one of the group's signature songs and a testament to Ruffin's immense talent.

Ruffin's impact extended beyond his vocal abilities. His charismatic stage presence and stylish persona added a new dimension to The Temptations' performances. He brought a sense of swagger and confidence that elevated their live shows, captivating audiences with his magnetic energy and undeniable charm. Ruffin's larger-than-life persona made him a natural focal point on stage, further solidifying his role as the group's frontman. However, Ruffin's time with The Temptations was not without its challenges. His growing ego and personal struggles strained his relationship with the group and ultimately led to his departure in 1968. Despite the challenges, Ruffin's contributions to The Temptations were undeniably significant, leaving an indelible mark on their musical legacy. His departure from The Temptations marked the beginning of a solo career that showcased his unique vocal prowess. Ruffin went on to achieve success as a solo artist, delivering memorable hits such as "Walk Away from Love" and "What Becomes of the Brokenhearted." Although he faced personal hardships and battled addiction throughout his life, Ruffin's impact as the lead singer of The Temptations remains an enduring part of music history.

David Ruffin's time with The Temptations was transformative for both the group and himself. His soul-stirring vocals and magnetic stage presence propelled the group to new heights of success and solidified their status as cultural icons. Ruffin's contributions to their sound and his undeniable talent as a performer helped shape the group's legacy and influenced generations of musicians to come.

The era of David Ruffin as the lead singer of The Temptations remains etched in the hearts of fans worldwide. His powerful voice, dynamic stage presence, and undeniable charisma continue to inspire and resonate with audiences, forever earning him a place in the pantheon of legendary performers.

Chapter 11: "My Girl": The First Taste of Success

In the annals of music history, there are certain songs that become timeless classics, forever etched in the hearts and minds of listeners. "My Girl," one of the most iconic and beloved songs of all time, stands as a testament to the incredible talent and artistic brilliance of The Temptations. This chapter delves into the creation and impact of "My Girl," the song that propelled The Temptations to new heights and forever changed the trajectory of their career.

In 1964, The Temptations were already gaining recognition with their earlier hits, but it was "My Girl" that would catapult them into mainstream success. The song was written by Smokey Robinson, a prolific songwriter and producer at

Motown Records, and Ronald White of The Miracles. Inspired by the love and devotion Robinson felt for his wife, the song became a timeless ode to the power of love.

From the opening notes of the distinctive guitar riff to the infectious melodies and heartfelt lyrics, "My Girl" captured the essence of romance and became an instant classic. The Temptations' flawless harmonies and David Ruffin's soul-stirring lead vocals brought the song to life, infusing it with an undeniable warmth and sincerity.

The song's lyrics painted a vivid picture of love's enduring nature, as the narrator expressed his unwavering affection for his special someone. Lines like "I've got sunshine on a cloudy day" and "I guess you'd say, what can make me feel this way? My girl" resonated with audiences, evoking feelings of joy, tenderness, and devotion.

Upon its release, "My Girl" quickly climbed the charts, reaching number one on the Billboard Hot 100 and becoming The Temptations' first chart-topping hit. Its universal appeal transcended genres and demographics, captivating listeners of all backgrounds. The song's success marked a turning point for the group, firmly establishing them as major players in the music industry.

Beyond its commercial success, "My Girl" became an anthem for lovers everywhere. Its timeless charm and heartfelt lyrics made it a go-to choice for weddings, anniversaries, and romantic moments. The song's enduring popularity has been reinforced by its inclusion in countless films, television shows, and advertisements, cementing its status as a cultural touchstone.

"My Girl" not only showcased The Temptations' exceptional vocal talents and their ability to craft exquisite harmonies but also paved the way for their future artistic endeavors. It set the stage for a string of hits that would follow, including "Ain't Too Proud to Beg," "I Wish It Would Rain," and "Papa Was a Rollin' Stone," solidifying their reputation as one of the most influential vocal groups of all time.

The impact of "My Girl" extended far beyond The Temptations' immediate success. It represented a milestone in the history of popular music, bridging the gap between R&B and mainstream audiences. The song's universal appeal showcased the power of soulful melodies and genuine emotion to transcend cultural boundaries and touch the hearts of listeners around the world.

Today, "My Girl" stands as an enduring testament to the timeless quality of The Temptations' music. Its infectious melodies, heartfelt lyrics, and soulful performances continue to captivate new generations, cementing its status as a true classic. The song remains a cherished part of The Temptations' legacy, reminding us of their extraordinary talent and the magic they created on stage and in the recording studio.

"My Girl" not only catapulted The Temptations to stardom but also left an indelible mark on the landscape of popular music. It is a timeless masterpiece that encapsulates the essence of love, joy, and the power of music to touch our souls.

Chapter 12: Hitting Their Stride: The Classic Temptations Sound

After their breakthrough with "My Girl," The Temptations entered a period of creative growth and exploration that solidified their signature sound. This chapter delves into the development of the classic Temptations sound, the result of their collaboration with renowned songwriters and producers, and the unique chemistry within the group.

With the departure of Elbridge "Al" Bryant and the addition of David Ruffin as their lead singer, The Temptations underwent a transformative period. They honed their vocal blend, refined their harmonies, and delved into a range of musical styles, ultimately defining the sound that would become their trademark.

At the heart of The Temptations' sound was the seamless integration of their individual voices. The group consisted of five distinct vocalists: David Ruffin, Eddie Kendricks, Paul Williams, Melvin Franklin, and Otis Williams. Each member brought a unique tone and style, yet together, their voices blended in perfect harmony. This synergy set them apart from other groups of the era and contributed to the richness and depth of their sound.

The Temptations' sound was further shaped by their collaborations with a stellar lineup of songwriters and producers at Motown Records. Artists like Smokey Robinson, Holland-Dozier-Holland, and Norman Whitfield understood the group's capabilities and crafted songs that showcased their vocal prowess. These collaborations resulted in a series of hits that would define The Temptations' legacy.

Motown's production techniques played a significant role in shaping the classic Temptations sound. The label's emphasis on polished arrangements, lush orchestration, and intricate vocal layering added a layer of sophistication to the group's recordings. This attention to detail enhanced the emotional impact of their songs and contributed to the timeless appeal of their music.

While The Temptations were known for their smooth ballads, they also explored a range of musical styles that showcased their versatility. They seamlessly transitioned from soulful love songs like "Just My Imagination (Running Away with Me)" to uptempo dance tracks like "Ain't Too Proud to Beg." This musical diversity allowed them to reach a broader audience and remain relevant in an ever-changing industry.

The influence of R&B, soul, gospel, and pop can be heard throughout The Temptations' discography. They infused their music with soulful melodies, intricate vocal arrangements, and emotionally charged performances. Whether singing about love, heartbreak, or social issues, The Temptations brought a depth of emotion and authenticity that resonated with listeners.

One of the defining elements of the classic Temptations sound was their ability to convey a range of emotions through their performances. They could evoke joy, longing, pain, and resilience within the span of a single song. This emotional depth, combined with their vocal precision, captivated audiences and solidified their status as true musical storytellers.

The Temptations' sound was not only defined by their musical abilities but also by their impeccable stage presence and synchronized choreography. Their coordinated dance moves and polished performances added a visual dimension to their live shows, elevating the overall experience for audiences.

As The Temptations continued to evolve, they embraced a more socially conscious approach to their music. Songs like "Ball of Confusion (That's What the World Is Today)" and "Papa Was a Rollin' Stone" tackled issues of social inequality, war, and the complexities of life. These powerful and thought-provoking tracks showcased the group's willingness to use their platform to address the pressing issues of their time.

The classic Temptations sound was a culmination of their vocal talents, their collaborations with Motown's finest songwriters and producers, and their ability to infuse their music with genuine emotion. It was a sound that resonated with audiences then and continues to do so today.

The Temptations' creative journey and their commitment to excellence resulted in a body of work that transcends generations. Their classic sound remains an enduring testament to their artistry and their ability to touch the hearts and souls of listeners around the world. The Temptations had indeed hit their stride, leaving an indelible mark on the world of music.

Chapter 13: Creative Tensions: Personalities within the Group

Behind the harmonious melodies and polished performances of The Temptations lay a dynamic interplay of personalities, each contributing to the group's creative journey. This chapter explores the creative tensions that arose within the group, the clash of egos, and how these dynamics both fueled their success and tested their unity.

With five distinct voices and strong individual identities, it was inevitable that creative tensions would emerge within The Temptations. Each member brought their own unique style and perspective, leading to a delicate balance of personalities and creative aspirations.

David Ruffin, with his powerful voice and commanding stage presence, often took the spotlight as the lead singer. His undeniable talent and growing ego sometimes created friction within the group. Ruffin's desire for greater creative control and his quest for solo success strained relationships and challenged the unity of the group.

Eddie Kendricks, known for his falsetto and smooth vocal style, also had a strong personality. He had a keen sense of musicality and brought a refined elegance to The Temptations' sound. Kendricks' creative input and desire to explore different musical directions sometimes clashed with the vision of other members, leading to tensions within the group.

Paul Williams, with his soulful voice and charismatic stage presence, was a vital part of The Temptations' success. However, his personal struggles with alcoholism and health issues added an additional layer of complexity to the group dynamics. While Williams was immensely talented, his difficulties impacted his ability to fully contribute to the creative process.

Melvin Franklin, the group's bass vocalist, brought a deep and resonant tone to their harmonies. He provided a solid foundation with his rich voice and steady presence. Franklin's calm and level-headed nature often served as a stabilizing force amidst the creative tensions that arose within the group.

Otis Williams, the group's de facto leader and the only original member remaining, played a pivotal role in managing the different personalities and maintaining the group's cohesion. Williams' diplomacy and ability to navigate the creative dynamics ensured that The Temptations stayed focused on their collective goal of making great music.

These creative tensions, while at times challenging, also fueled The Temptations' success. The clash of egos pushed each member to elevate their performances and contribute their best to the group's collective sound. The resulting blend of voices, styles, and personalities created a unique and captivating musical experience.

However, the tensions within the group also took a toll. The struggles with egos, substance abuse, and personal issues strained relationships and affected the overall harmony of the group. These challenges ultimately led to lineup changes and shifts in the group's dynamic over the years.

Despite the internal struggles, The Temptations managed to maintain their commitment to excellence and deliver exceptional music to their fans. Their ability to transcend their personal differences and come together on stage was a testament to their professionalism and dedication to their craft.

In the face of creative tensions, The Temptations continued to evolve and adapt. They navigated the changing landscape of the music industry, embraced new musical influences, and explored different genres. This resilience and willingness to embrace change allowed them to remain relevant and influential throughout their career.

The creative tensions within The Temptations were not just a source of conflict but also a catalyst for growth and artistic exploration. The clash of personalities and the pursuit of individual creative visions pushed the group to continually push boundaries and strive for greatness.

Ultimately, it was the delicate balance of these personalities, with all their complexities and conflicts, that contributed to the distinct sound and enduring legacy of The Temptations. Their ability to harness their individual talents and channel them into a collective vision remains a testament to their artistry and the lasting impact they made on the music industry.

Chapter 14: Motown Family: Working with Berry Gordy and the Label.

The Temptations' journey to stardom would not have been possible without their partnership with Motown Records and its visionary founder, Berry

Gordy. This chapter explores the unique relationship between The Temptations and the Motown family, the influence of Berry Gordy, and the impact of the label on their career.

Motown Records, founded by Berry Gordy in 1959, was more than just a record label. It was a musical movement that revolutionized the industry and left an indelible mark on popular music. Gordy's vision was to create a company that would produce music that appealed to all audiences, regardless of race or background. This vision resonated with The Temptations, as they sought to reach a diverse fan base with their music.

The relationship between The Temptations and Motown was built on trust, mutual respect, and a shared commitment to excellence. Berry Gordy recognized the immense talent of The Temptations and worked closely with them to cultivate their sound and shape their artistic direction. He provided the guidance, resources, and support needed for the group to flourish.

Motown Records, often referred to as "Hitsville U.S.A.," was a creative hub where artists and songwriters came together to create magic. The label's unique approach involved a collaborative process, with artists working alongside a team of songwriters, producers, and arrangers to craft their music. The Temptations were immersed in this creative environment, collaborating with some of the industry's most talented individuals.

Berry Gordy's hands-on involvement extended beyond the business side of things. He served as a mentor and coach to The Temptations, helping them refine their stage presence, develop their image, and navigate the challenges of the industry. Gordy's keen eye for talent and his ability to recognize the potential of each artist allowed him to guide The Temptations towards their greatest successes.

Motown's production team, including the renowned songwriting and producing trio Holland-Dozier-Holland, played a crucial role in shaping The Temptations' sound. They worked closely with the group to create songs that showcased their unique vocal blend and brought out the best in each member. Motown's commitment to quality and attention to detail resulted in the timeless hits that became synonymous with The Temptations' legacy.

The Motown family was more than just a label; it was a supportive community of artists. The Temptations found themselves surrounded by talented peers, including The Supremes, Stevie Wonder, and Marvin Gaye, among others. The camaraderie and friendly competition among these artists pushed everyone to strive for greatness and elevate their craft.

Motown's impact went beyond the music itself. The label's commitment to social change and breaking down racial barriers resonated with The Temptations, who used their platform to advocate for equality and justice. Through their music, The Temptations became a voice for their generation, addressing social issues and inspiring change.

The collaboration between The Temptations and Motown Records resulted in a string of hits that defined an era. From "My Girl" to "Papa Was a Rollin' Stone," these songs became anthems that transcended time and captured the essence of their generation. Motown's marketing and promotion strategies ensured that The Temptations' music reached audiences around the world, solidifying their status as one of the most successful and influential groups of their time.

The bond between The Temptations and the Motown family extended beyond their time together. Decades later, the Motown legacy continues to be celebrated, and the music of The Temptations remains a testament to the enduring power of their partnership with the label.

Working with Berry Gordy and the Motown family was a pivotal chapter in The Temptations' career. The support, guidance, and collaborative spirit of the label allowed the group to fully realize their potential and create music that touched the hearts of millions. The Motown family became an integral part of The Temptations' story, shaping their sound, amplifying their voices, and cementing their place in music history.

Chapter 15: A Series of Hits: Dominating the Charts

With their impeccable vocal harmonies, electrifying performances, and an unwavering commitment to excellence, The Temptations embarked on a remarkable journey that led to a series of chart-topping hits. This chapter explores their unprecedented success, their domination of the charts, and the impact of their music on popular culture.

Following their breakthrough with "My Girl," The Temptations experienced an extraordinary run of hit records that solidified their status as one of the most successful groups of their time. Their unique blend of soulful melodies, captivating performances, and timeless lyrics resonated with audiences across the globe.

The string of hits began with "Ain't Too Proud to Beg," a gritty and energetic track that showcased The Temptations' versatility and their ability to captivate listeners with their raw and powerful sound. The song quickly climbed the charts, cementing their place as soul music pioneers. Next came "I Wish It Would Rain," a poignant ballad that showcased the group's ability to convey deep emotion and vulnerability through their music. With its heartfelt lyrics and soul-stirring performances, the song struck a chord with audiences and further solidified The Temptations' place in the music industry.

The Temptations' chart domination continued with "Cloud Nine," a groundbreaking track that marked a departure from their traditional sound. With its psychedelic funk influences and socially conscious lyrics, "Cloud Nine" showcased the group's willingness to experiment and push musical boundaries. The song earned them their first Grammy Award and further expanded their fan base.

Perhaps one of their most iconic hits, "Papa Was a Rollin' Stone," became an instant classic. With its hypnotic bassline, haunting melodies, and introspective lyrics, the song exemplified The Temptations' ability to create immersive musical experiences. "Papa Was a Rollin' Stone" topped the charts and became a cultural phenomenon, solidifying the group's place as musical trailblazers. Throughout their career, The Temptations continued to dominate the charts with hits like "Just My Imagination (Running Away with Me)," "Get Ready," and "Ball of Confusion (That's What the World Is Today)." These songs showcased their versatility, vocal prowess, and their ability to connect with audiences on a profound level.

The impact of The Temptations' music extended far beyond the charts. Their songs served as the soundtrack of a generation, capturing the essence of the social and cultural shifts of the time. Their music became anthems for love, resilience, and social change, resonating with listeners of all backgrounds.

The Temptations' success was not only a testament to their talent but also to their ability to adapt and evolve with the changing musical landscape. They embraced new styles, incorporated innovative production techniques, and continued to push the boundaries of their sound. This adaptability allowed them to maintain their relevance and appeal to audiences across generations.

Their chart dominance was further enhanced by their electrifying live performances. The Temptations' energetic choreography, impeccable harmonies, and dynamic stage presence captivated audiences around the world. Their live shows became legendary, leaving a lasting impact on those fortunate enough to witness their electrifying performances.

The Temptations' series of hits not only propelled them to the top of the charts but also solidified their place in music history. They became a blueprint for success, inspiring countless artists who followed in their footsteps. Their influence can still be heard in the music of today, as their iconic sound continues to resonate with new generations of listeners.

The Temptations' domination of the charts was a testament to their talent, their artistic vision, and their unwavering dedication to their craft. Their songs have stood the test of time, remaining as beloved today as they were when they first hit the airwaves. The Temptations' journey to the top of the charts was a remarkable achievement that solidified their place as legends in the world of music.

Chapter 16: The Temptations and the Changing Musical Landscape.

As the music industry evolved and the cultural landscape shifted, The Temptations found themselves navigating through a changing musical landscape. This chapter explores how the group adapted to new styles, embraced musical experimentation, and continued to leave an indelible mark on popular music.

Throughout their career, The Temptations were known for their signature sound, characterized by rich harmonies, soulful melodies, and timeless lyrics. However, as the 1970s approached, the music scene underwent a transformation. Funk, disco, and other genres emerged, pushing boundaries and challenging traditional soundscapes.

The Temptations recognized the need to adapt and embrace new musical styles while staying true to their core identity. They ventured into funk with songs like "Cloud Nine" and "Ball of Confusion (That's What the World Is Today)," infusing their classic sound with funk-inspired rhythms and socially conscious lyrics. This foray into funk not only resonated with audiences but also demonstrated their versatility as artists.

As the disco era gained momentum, The Temptations incorporated elements of the genre into their music. Songs like "Shakey Ground" and

"Power" showcased their ability to incorporate infectious dance beats while maintaining their soulful essence. Their willingness to evolve and explore new sonic territories allowed them to remain relevant and connected with changing audiences.

Despite embracing new musical influences, The Temptations never abandoned their roots. They continued to release ballads and romantic songs, such as "Just My Imagination (Running Away with Me)" and "I'm Gonna Make You Love Me," which showcased their ability to convey heartfelt emotions with grace and authenticity. These timeless ballads demonstrated their enduring appeal and ability to capture the essence of love and longing.

The Temptations also collaborated with a diverse range of artists, further expanding their musical horizons. They joined forces with contemporary artists such as Rick James, who produced their hit song "Standing on the Top." This collaboration bridged the gap between generations and showcased their ability to seamlessly blend their classic sound with modern production techniques. The group's ability to adapt to the changing musical landscape was not only a testament to their talent but also to their willingness to take risks. They were unafraid to step outside their comfort zone and experiment with new sounds, styles, and collaborations. This willingness to evolve allowed them to maintain their relevance and appeal to a broader audience.

Furthermore, The Temptations' impact on the changing musical landscape extended beyond their own music. Their influence could be heard in the work of artists who followed in their footsteps. The harmonies, choreography, and stage presence that defined The Temptations became a blueprint for future generations of performers.

As the 1980s and beyond arrived, The Temptations continued to release music, tour, and captivate audiences. Their resilience and ability to adapt in the face of a changing musical landscape ensured their longevity and enduring legacy.

The Temptations' ability to navigate the changing musical landscape was a testament to their artistry and dedication. They embraced new styles, incorporated innovative elements, and continued to deliver music that resonated with audiences. Their willingness to evolve while staying true to their core identity solidified their status as icons of popular music, leaving an indelible mark on the ever-changing musical landscape.

Chapter 17: Psychedelic Soul: Experimenting with New Sounds

In the late 1960s, a wave of musical experimentation swept through the music industry, giving rise to a genre known as psychedelic soul. This chapter explores how The Temptations, always on the forefront of musical innovation, embraced this new sound and ventured into uncharted territories.

Psychedelic soul blended elements of traditional soul music with the psychedelic rock sounds that were popular at the time. It was characterized by its fusion of soulful vocals, intricate instrumentation, and mind-bending psychedelic influences. The Temptations, known for their rich harmonies and captivating performances, were eager to explore this new sonic landscape.

The group's exploration into psychedelic soul began with their groundbreaking album, "Cloud Nine," released in 1969. Produced by Norman Whitfield, the album showcased a departure from their traditional sound, incorporating elements of funk, rock, and psychedelic influences. The title track, "Cloud Nine," was a bold departure from their earlier work, featuring a driving bassline, distorted guitars, and socially conscious lyrics. It became their first Grammy-winning hit and set the stage for their venture into the realm of psychedelic soul. Building on the success of "Cloud Nine," The Temptations released their landmark album, "Puzzle People," in 1969. The album continued to explore the boundaries of psychedelic soul, with tracks like "I Can't Get Next to You" and "Don't Let the Joneses Get You Down." These songs featured intricate arrangements, innovative production techniques, and a fusion of soulful vocals with psychedelic instrumentations, creating a sound that was both mesmerizing and groundbreaking.

The Temptations' exploration of psychedelic soul reached its pinnacle with the release of "Psychedelic Shack" in 1970. The title track, along with songs like "Ball of Confusion (That's What the World Is Today)" and "Hum Along and Dance," showcased the group's willingness to push musical boundaries and experiment with unconventional sounds. These tracks featured swirling melodies, psychedelic guitar riffs, and thought-provoking lyrics that reflected the social and cultural climate of the time.

Their venture into psychedelic soul was not without risks. Some fans were initially taken aback by the departure from their classic sound. However, The Temptations' boldness and artistic vision paid off, as their psychedelic soul sound resonated with a new generation of listeners and expanded their fan base.

The collaboration between The Temptations and producer Norman Whitfield was instrumental in shaping their psychedelic soul sound. Whitfield's innovative production techniques and willingness to experiment allowed the group to fully explore the potential of this new genre. His visionary approach, coupled with The Temptations' exceptional vocal abilities, resulted in a series of groundbreaking albums that pushed the boundaries of soul music. The impact of The Temptations' psychedelic soul era extended beyond their own discography. Their experimentation and success paved the way for other artists to explore the possibilities of blending soul and psychedelic influences. The genre itself left an indelible mark on the music industry, influencing subsequent generations of musicians and continuing to inspire new sounds and creative approaches.

While The Temptations would later evolve and explore other musical styles, their foray into psychedelic soul remains a defining chapter in their career. It showcased their fearlessness, artistic growth, and willingness to embrace new sounds. The group's ability to seamlessly merge their soulful harmonies with the psychedelic elements of the era solidified their status as musical innovators and further cemented their place in music history.

Chapter 18: The Norman Whitfield Collaboration: A Revolutionary Shift

The collaboration between The Temptations and producer Norman Whitfield marked a revolutionary shift in their musical direction and sound. This chapter explores the transformative partnership that pushed the boundaries of soul music, solidified The Temptations' legacy, and left an indelible mark on popular music.

Norman Whitfield, a talented songwriter and producer, recognized the immense potential of The Temptations and saw an opportunity to create something truly groundbreaking. Together, they embarked on a creative journey that would redefine the sound of soul music and catapult the group to new heights of success.

Whitfield's visionary approach to production and songwriting introduced a more cinematic and dramatic sound to The Temptations' repertoire. He sought to capture the essence of the times, infusing their music with social commentary and introspective lyrics that reflected the realities of the era.

The collaboration yielded a string of hits that pushed the boundaries of soul music. Songs like "Cloud Nine," "Runaway Child, Running Wild," and "Psychedelic Shack" showcased a fusion of soul, funk, and psychedelic influences. These tracks were characterized by their intricate arrangements, innovative production techniques, and thought-provoking lyrics. Whitfield's distinctive production style, which often incorporated psychedelic instrumentations, created a sonic landscape that was both adventurous and captivating.

One of the most notable aspects of the collaboration was the way it allowed each member of The Temptations to shine individually. Whitfield recognized the unique strengths and vocal abilities of each member and crafted songs that showcased their individual talents while maintaining the group's signature harmonies. This approach added depth and dimension to their music, making each track a masterclass in vocal performance.

The collaboration between Whitfield and The Temptations reached its apex with the release of the album "Masterpiece" in 1973. The album featured epic compositions such as the title track, a sprawling masterpiece that showcased the group's vocal prowess and Whitfield's intricate production techniques. It was a culmination of their collective creativity and musical vision.

However, as with any artistic collaboration, tensions arose. The ambitious nature of Whitfield's production style sometimes clashed with the traditionalist views of some members of the group. These creative differences led to occasional conflicts, but ultimately, the collaboration pushed The Temptations to new artistic heights and solidified their status as innovators within the music industry.

The impact of the collaboration between The Temptations and Norman Whitfield extended far beyond their immediate success. Their revolutionary sound inspired and influenced countless artists across various genres. The fusion of soul, funk, and psychedelic elements paved the way for the development of funk music as a genre and left an indelible mark on popular music as a whole.

The Norman Whitfield collaboration not only transformed The Temptations' sound but also furthered their relevance in an ever-evolving music industry. It showcased their willingness to embrace experimentation, their commitment to social commentary, and their ability to evolve and adapt to changing musical landscapes.

While the collaboration eventually came to an end, the impact of their work together remains an integral part of The Temptations' legacy. It solidified their status as musical pioneers, pushed the boundaries of soul music, and elevated their artistry to new heights. The collaboration between The Temptations and Norman Whitfield will forever be remembered as a revolutionary shift that changed the course of their careers and left an indelible mark on the history of popular music.

Chapter 19: Paul Williams: The Unsung Hero

Within the legendary lineup of The Temptations, one member stood out as an unsung hero whose contributions were essential to the group's success. This chapter explores the life and impact of Paul Williams, a talented vocalist and performer whose contributions to The Temptations cannot be overstated.

Born on July 2, 1939, in Birmingham, Alabama, Paul Williams grew up immersed in gospel music. His powerful and soulful voice quickly caught the attention of those around him. Williams possessed a captivating stage presence and an ability to connect with audiences on a profound level. Little did he know that his talent would lead him to become an integral part of one of the most iconic vocal groups in music history.

Paul Williams joined The Temptations in 1960, becoming the group's baritone and occasional lead singer. While his vocal range and abilities were impressive, his contributions extended far beyond his singing talent. Williams was a master of choreography, known for his smooth moves and precise footwork on stage. He played a pivotal role in creating the group's iconic dance routines and polished performances.

More than just a performer, Williams was also a mentor and guide for the younger members of the group. His experience and wisdom provided invaluable support as they navigated the challenges and pressures of the music industry. Williams was respected and admired by his fellow group members, who often turned to him for guidance and advice.

Despite his immense talent and contributions, Paul Williams struggled with personal demons. He battled alcoholism, which affected his health and impacted his ability to perform. As his struggles intensified, he made the difficult decision to step back from the spotlight, but his legacy within The Temptations endured.

Williams' impact on The Temptations' sound cannot be overstated. His rich and soulful baritone voice added depth and texture to the group's harmonies, creating a signature sound that resonated with audiences worldwide. His lead vocal performances, such as "Don't Look Back" and "For Once in My Life," showcased his versatility and ability to convey emotion with sincerity.

Tragically, Paul Williams' life was cut short. On August 17, 1973, at the age of 34, he was found dead in his Detroit home, the result of a self-inflicted gunshot wound. His death was a devastating loss for The Temptations and the music community as a whole. It marked the end of an era and left a void that could never be filled.

Despite his untimely passing, Paul Williams' contributions to The Temptations continue to be celebrated and cherished. His impact on the group's sound, choreography, and mentorship remains an integral part of their legacy. His talent, dedication, and artistry made an indelible mark on the world of music, and his influence can still be heard in the performances of The Temptations to this day.

While Paul Williams may be an unsung hero in the grand narrative of The Temptations' success, his legacy lives on as a testament to the profound impact one individual can have within a legendary group. His voice, his moves, and his guiding presence will forever be remembered, ensuring that his role as an unsung hero of The Temptations is never forgotten.

Chapter 20: The Temptations' Live Shows: Captivating Audiences

One of the hallmarks of The Temptations' enduring success was their ability to captivate audiences through their electrifying live performances. This chapter explores the dynamic and captivating nature of The Temptations' live shows, which brought their music to life and solidified their status as one of the greatest live acts in music history.

From the moment the curtains opened and The Temptations took the stage, a palpable energy filled the air. The group's synchronized dance moves, impeccable harmonies, and charismatic stage presence combined to create an unforgettable live experience. Their performances were a testament to the group's dedication to perfection and their commitment to delivering an extraordinary show every time they stepped on stage.

Central to The Temptations' live shows was their choreography, which became an iconic element of their performances. With precision and grace, they executed intricate dance routines that were visually captivating and perfectly synchronized. The group's cohesive movements added an extra layer of spectacle to their performances, elevating their music to a whole new level.

In addition to their exceptional choreography, The Temptations' vocal performances were nothing short of extraordinary. Their harmonies were flawless, weaving together in a tapestry of soulful melodies. Each member's voice brought a unique texture and color to the group's sound, creating a harmonious blend that resonated with audiences. Their ability to deliver pitch-perfect vocals while executing complex dance routines demonstrated their remarkable talent and professionalism.

The Temptations' live shows were not simply a recitation of their recorded songs; they were transformative experiences that allowed the group to connect with their audience on a profound level. Through their dynamic stage presence and heartfelt performances, they created an atmosphere that brought their music to life in a way that studio recordings simply could not replicate.

Another key element of The Temptations' live shows was their interaction with the audience. They engaged with the crowd, captivating them with their charm and wit. Whether it was a playful banter between songs or inviting the audience to participate in their choreography, they made sure that everyone felt like an integral part of the experience. This connection between the group and their fans created an electric atmosphere that made each show feel like a shared celebration. The Temptations' live performances were renowned for their energy and showmanship. They were masters of pacing and knew how to build anticipation throughout their setlist, delivering a mix of high-energy numbers, tender ballads, and crowd-pleasing hits. Each performance was meticulously crafted to take the audience on an emotional journey, leaving them exhilarated and wanting more.

Beyond the music and the spectacle, The Temptations' live shows were also a testament to their professionalism and dedication to their craft. They consistently delivered polished performances, maintaining their high standards and pushing themselves to exceed expectations. Their commitment to excellence was evident in every note sung, every dance move executed, and every moment spent on stage.

The impact of The Temptations' live shows extended far beyond the concert venues. Their reputation as a captivating live act solidified their status as cultural icons and earned them a dedicated fan base that spanned generations. Their performances continue to inspire and influence artists today, setting the bar for what it means to deliver an unforgettable live experience.

The Temptations' live shows were a testament to their artistry, talent, and ability to create an immersive musical experience. Through their choreography, vocals, and engagement with the audience, they captivated audiences and left an indelible mark on the world of live performance. Their shows were not mere concerts; they were transformative moments that exemplified the power of music and the enduring legacy of The Temptations.

Chapter 21: Challenges and Personal Struggles

Behind the glitz and glamour of their success, The Temptations faced their fair share of challenges and personal struggles. This chapter delves into the trials and tribulations that tested the group's unity, resilience, and individual members.

As with any long-lasting musical group, The Temptations experienced internal conflicts and tensions that stemmed from the pressures of fame, creative differences, and personal ambitions. The combination of strong personalities and the pursuit of individual aspirations occasionally led to clashes within the group. These challenges were magnified by the demanding nature of their rigorous touring schedule, the constant spotlight, and the ever-evolving music industry.

One of the major challenges The Temptations faced was navigating the changing musical landscape. As the 1960s progressed, new genres and styles emerged, shifting popular tastes and posing a threat to the group's relevance. The rise of psychedelic rock, funk, and other contemporary genres presented challenges for the group as they sought to adapt their sound and maintain their commercial success.

Moreover, the group's personal struggles added another layer of complexity to their journey. Some members grappled with substance abuse, mental health issues, and the pressures of fame. These personal battles often spilled over into their professional lives, affecting their performances, relationships within the group, and their overall well-being.

One of the most notable examples of personal struggle within The Temptations was the tragic story of Paul Williams. As mentioned earlier, Williams battled alcoholism, which impacted his health and ultimately led to his untimely death. His struggles, while deeply personal, had an undeniable effect on the group as a whole, both creatively and emotionally.

The individual members of The Temptations also faced personal challenges and aspirations outside of the group. Some sought solo careers, yearning for recognition and success beyond their collective achievements. While these ambitions were understandable, they often created tensions within the group, challenging the delicate balance between individual aspirations and the unity of The Temptations as a whole.

Despite these challenges, The Temptations persevered. They navigated the ups and downs of their personal struggles and managed to maintain their collective vision and commitment to their music. Their deep-rooted friendships, shared history, and mutual respect provided the foundation upon which they could weather the storms that came their way.

Overcoming these challenges required compromise, understanding, and a commitment to the greater good of the group. The Temptations learned to harness their collective strength and harness their creative differences to fuel their growth and evolution. They embraced the changes in the music industry, experimented with new sounds, and reinvented themselves to stay relevant.

Ultimately, it was the unwavering dedication and resilience of The Temptations that allowed them to overcome their challenges and continue their musical journey. Their ability to rise above personal struggles and maintain their bond as a group ensured their enduring legacy and impact on the world of music.

The challenges and personal struggles faced by The Temptations serve as a reminder that behind the curtain of fame, artists are human beings with their own battles and vulnerabilities. It is a testament to their strength, unity, and love for their craft that they persevered and continued to create timeless music that resonates with audiences to this day. The trials they faced along the way only added depth to their story and further solidified their status as icons of resilience and determination.

Chapter 22: Dennis Edwards: A New Frontman Emerges

In the ever-evolving journey of The Temptations, a pivotal moment arrived when a new frontman emerged, bringing a fresh energy and vocal prowess to the group. This chapter explores the arrival of Dennis Edwards, a talented singer who revitalized The Temptations and helped propel them to new heights.

Born on February 3, 1943, in Fairfield, Alabama, Dennis Edwards grew up immersed in gospel music, honing his vocal skills and developing a soulful and powerful voice. His talent and charisma caught the attention of Motown Records, who recognized his potential and invited him to audition for The Temptations.

In 1968, Dennis Edwards officially joined The Temptations as their new lead vocalist, replacing the departing David Ruffin. Edwards brought a distinctive and captivating vocal style to the group, characterized by his gritty and impassioned delivery. His voice, infused with raw emotion, added a new dimension to The Temptations' sound, captivating audiences and reinvigorating the group's music.

With Edwards at the helm, The Temptations embarked on a new musical direction. Their sound evolved to incorporate elements of funk, reflecting the changing landscape of popular music at the time. Edwards' soulful and dynamic vocals were perfectly suited to this new direction, infusing the group's music with a fresh energy and intensity.

One of the defining moments of Edwards' tenure with The Temptations was the release of the hit single "Cloud Nine" in 1968. The song, produced by Norman Whitfield, showcased Edwards' powerful vocals and set the stage for the group's exploration of socially conscious and politically charged themes. "Cloud Nine" marked a shift in The Temptations' music, embracing a more socially aware and progressive approach that resonated with audiences of the time.

Edwards' impact extended beyond his vocal contributions. He brought a captivating stage presence and energy to The Temptations' live performances, captivating audiences with his charismatic and soulful delivery. His chemistry with the other group members was palpable, as they seamlessly harmonized and complemented each other's talents.

However, Edwards' time with The Temptations was not without its challenges. The group faced internal conflicts and tensions, partly due to the shift in their musical direction and creative differences. These challenges tested the unity of the group but also pushed them to grow and evolve as artists.

Despite the challenges, Edwards' tenure with The Temptations produced a string of successful albums and hit singles. Songs like "Papa Was a Rollin' Stone," "Ball of Confusion," and "Just My Imagination (Running Away with Me)" showcased Edwards' vocal range and ability to convey emotion with depth and authenticity. These songs became timeless classics, solidifying The Temptations' status as one of the greatest vocal groups in music history.

Dennis Edwards' contribution to The Temptations cannot be overstated. His powerful and soulful voice, combined with his stage presence and passion, reenergized the group and helped them navigate the changing musical landscape of the 1960s and 1970s. His impact on the group's sound and direction revitalized their career and allowed them to continue evolving and reaching new audiences.

Tragically, Dennis Edwards' time with The Temptations was cut short. After leaving the group in 1977, he pursued a solo career and continued to make music, but his impact as the new frontman of The Temptations remains indelible. He passed away on February 1, 2018, leaving behind a lasting legacy and a body of work that continues to inspire and resonate with fans around the world.

Dennis Edwards' arrival marked a significant chapter in the story of The Temptations. His talent, vocal prowess, and charismatic presence injected new life into the group, solidifying their position as pioneers of soul music. His contributions, both on stage and in the studio, helped shape the sound and legacy of The Temptations, leaving an indelible mark on the history of popular music.

Chapter 23: Political Commentary: "Ball of Confusion" and "Papa Was a Rollin' Stone."

The Temptations' music not only showcased their incredible vocal talents but also served as a platform for social and political commentary. This chapter focuses on two iconic songs, "Ball of Confusion" and "Papa Was a Rollin' Stone," which exemplify The Temptations' ability to address pressing issues of their time and resonate with audiences on a deeper level.

Released in 1970, "Ball of Confusion (That's What the World Is Today)" became an anthem of its era, capturing the chaotic and tumultuous nature of the late 1960s and early 1970s. Written by Norman Whitfield and Barrett Strong, the song's lyrics painted a vivid picture of the social, political, and cultural upheaval occurring around the world.

"Ball of Confusion" dissected the complexities and contradictions of society, touching on issues such as racial tension, war, drug abuse, and environmental concerns. The song's powerful and thought-provoking lyrics reflected the frustrations and uncertainties of the time, giving voice to the collective concerns and anxieties of a generation. With its infectious funk-infused sound and socially conscious lyrics, "Ball of Confusion" struck a chord with audiences. It reached the top of the charts and became one of The Temptations' signature songs, resonating with listeners who sought a deeper understanding of the world around them.

Another notable example of The Temptations' political commentary can be found in "Papa Was a Rollin' Stone," released in 1972. The song, written by Norman Whitfield and Barrett Strong, delved into the complexities of family, abandonment, and the consequences of one's actions.

"Papa Was a Rollin' Stone" tells the story of a young man who grows up in the absence of a father figure, as his father leads a life of transience and irresponsibility. The song's lyrics, delivered with haunting intensity by the group, paint a vivid picture of a fractured family and the lasting impact of a father's choices on his children.

Beyond its narrative, "Papa Was a Rollin' Stone" also carried a broader social commentary. The lyrics explored themes of poverty, urban decay, and the systemic issues that perpetuated cycles of hardship and struggle. The song's emotional depth, combined with its infectious groove, created a powerful and unforgettable musical experience.

Both "Ball of Confusion" and "Papa Was a Rollin' Stone" showcased The Temptations' willingness to address pressing societal issues through their music. These songs went beyond traditional love ballads, delving into the complexities of the world they lived in and offering a critical lens through which listeners could view and reflect upon their own lives.

The Temptations' ability to infuse their music with political and social commentary demonstrated their commitment to using their platform to provoke thought, spark conversations, and inspire change. Through their thought-provoking lyrics and soul-stirring performances, they provided a voice for the marginalized, shed light on injustices, and contributed to the cultural and political conversations of their time.

"Ball of Confusion" and "Papa Was a Rollin' Stone" remain timeless classics, testaments to The Temptations' enduring impact and relevance. These songs transcended their initial era, continuing to resonate with audiences across generations. They serve as a reminder of the power of music to not only entertain but also inspire and prompt reflection on the world we live in.

The Temptations' ability to infuse their music with political and social commentary demonstrated their commitment to using their platform to provoke thought, spark conversations, and inspire change. Through their thought-provoking lyrics and soul-stirring performances, they provided a voice for the marginalized, shed light on injustices, and contributed to the cultural and political conversations of their time.

"Ball of Confusion" and "Papa Was a Rollin' Stone" remain timeless classics, testaments to The Temptations' enduring impact and relevance. These songs transcended their initial era, continuing to resonate with audiences across generations. They serve as a reminder of the power of music to not only entertain but also inspire and prompt reflection on the world we live in.

Chapter 24: The Temptations in the 1970s: Evolving Image and Sound

As the 1970s dawned, The Temptations found themselves navigating a changing musical landscape and undergoing significant transformations both in their image and sound. This chapter explores the group's evolution during this period, as they continued to captivate audiences with their unique blend of soul, funk, and R&B. With the departure of Dennis Edwards in 1977, The Temptations faced the challenge of finding a new lead vocalist who could fill the void left by his departure. Damon Harris, previously a member of The Young Vandals, stepped into the role, bringing his smooth tenor voice to the group. Harris' addition marked a shift in the group's sound, as they embraced a more polished and harmonious style. During the 1970s, The Temptations' music evolved to incorporate elements of funk, disco, and psychedelic soul, reflecting the changing trends and influences of the era. They collaborated with renowned producer Norman Whitfield, who played a significant role in shaping their sound during this period. Whitfield's innovative production techniques and incorporation of synthesizers and extended instrumental breaks added a new dimension to The Temptations' music.

The group's image also underwent a transformation in the 1970s. They embraced flamboyant stage attire, featuring matching suits, colorful outfits, and stylish accessories. This visual evolution mirrored the broader trends of the time, as artists began to experiment with their appearance and embrace a more extravagant and individualistic style.

One of the standout albums from this period was "A Song for You" (1975), which showcased The Temptations' versatility and musical dexterity. The album featured a mix of soulful ballads, energetic dance tracks, and socially conscious songs. Tracks like "Shakey Ground" and "Glasshouse" displayed The Temptations' ability to blend their classic harmonies with the funk-infused sounds of the 1970s.

As the decade progressed, The Temptations faced both commercial successes and challenges. They scored hits with songs like "Masterpiece" and "Happy People," which showcased their ability to adapt to the changing musical landscape while maintaining their signature harmonies and soulful delivery.

However, internal conflicts and personnel changes continued to affect the group. Damon Harris departed in 1975, and his replacement, Glenn Leonard, brought a new vocal dynamic to the group. The ever-shifting lineup presented its own set of challenges, but The Temptations persevered, determined to continue their musical journey.

Despite the changes and challenges, The Temptations remained a force to be reckoned with on the live performance circuit. Their captivating stage presence, synchronized choreography, and soul-stirring vocals continued to mesmerize audiences around the world. Their performances were a testament to their enduring talent and dedication to delivering a memorable and entertaining show.

The 1970s marked a period of evolution and growth for The Temptations. They embraced new musical influences, experimented with different sounds, and adapted to the ever-changing trends of the time.

While their lineup may have shifted, their commitment to delivering top-notch performances and timeless music remained unwavering.

As the decade drew to a close, The Temptations looked ahead to the next chapter in their storied career. Little did they know that their legacy would endure, cementing their status as one of the greatest vocal groups in the history of popular music.

Chapter 25: Personnel Changes: Departures and Arrivals

Throughout their storied career, The Temptations experienced several personnel changes, with members coming and going, leaving an indelible impact on the group's dynamic and sound. This chapter delves into the departures and arrivals that shaped The Temptations' journey, highlighting the resilience and adaptability of the group.

One of the most significant departures in The Temptations' history occurred in 1968 when David Ruffin, the group's charismatic lead singer, left the ensemble. Ruffin's departure marked the end of an era, as his distinctive voice and stage presence had become synonymous with The Temptations' early successes. His departure, though heartbreaking for fans, opened the door for new talent to join the group.

Following Ruffin's departure, The Temptations welcomed Dennis Edwards as their new lead vocalist. Edwards brought a powerful and soulful voice that revitalized the group, propelling them in a new musical direction. Edwards' addition marked the beginning of a new chapter for The Temptations and demonstrated their ability to adapt to change while maintaining their signature sound.

In the 1970s, The Temptations experienced a series of personnel changes. Damon Harris, who had joined the group as a replacement for Paul Williams, left in 1975. His departure led to the arrival of Glenn Leonard, whose smooth tenor voice became a prominent element of The Temptations' sound during this period.

Another notable departure came in 1977 when Dennis Edwards left the group to pursue a solo career. While his exit marked the end of an era, The Temptations once again embarked on the search for a new lead vocalist to fill the void left by Edwards. Damon Harris briefly returned to the group before being replaced by Louis Price, who brought his own unique vocal style and energy to the ensemble.

Throughout the years, The Temptations also saw changes in the lineup beyond the lead vocalists. Original member and founding bass singer Melvin Franklin departed in 1994, and his place was filled by Harry McGilberry. Later, in 2003, Terry Weeks replaced Ray Davis as the group's high tenor. Despite the ever-changing roster, The Temptations maintained their commitment to excellence and continued to captivate audiences with their harmonies, choreography, and stage presence. Each new member brought their own talent and contributed to the group's evolving sound, ensuring that The Temptations' legacy endured.

While personnel changes presented challenges, The Temptations' resilience and ability to adapt allowed them to navigate these transitions and remain at the forefront of the music industry. The group's enduring popularity is a testament to their ability to blend individual talents into a cohesive and dynamic whole.

The Temptations' personnel changes demonstrated the group's willingness to evolve and embrace new voices, ensuring their music remained fresh and relevant. Each departure and arrival marked a new chapter in the group's history, showcasing the ever-changing nature of their journey while preserving the essence of The Temptations' unmistakable sound.

As The Temptations' story continued to unfold, their personnel changes would serve as a testament to the group's enduring spirit and their commitment to creating timeless music that resonated with audiences around the world.

Chapter 26: Personal Struggles: Substance Abuse and Mental Health.

Behind the scenes of The Temptations' remarkable success and captivating performances, the group members faced personal struggles, including battles with substance abuse and mental health issues. This chapter sheds light on the challenges they encountered and the impact these struggles had on their lives and careers.

Like many artists of their time, The Temptations were not immune to the temptations and pressures that came with fame and success. Some members of the group turned to substance abuse as a means of coping with the demands of their rigorous schedules, the weight of expectations, and the personal challenges they faced.

One of the most well-known instances of substance abuse within the group was David Ruffin's battle with drug addiction. Ruffin's addiction began to take a toll on his personal life and his relationship with his fellow bandmates. Despite his undeniable talent, his substance abuse issues led to tensions and conflicts within the group, ultimately resulting in his departure in 1968.

The struggles with substance abuse extended beyond Ruffin. Dennis Edwards, while serving as the lead vocalist, also battled addiction throughout his tenure with The Temptations. His substance abuse issues at times affected his ability to fulfill his responsibilities within the group. Despite the challenges, Edwards made efforts to seek help and eventually overcame his addiction.

The impact of substance abuse on The Temptations was not limited to the lead vocalists. Several other members of the group, including Paul Williams and Melvin Franklin, also struggled with addiction. These personal battles often affected their performances, relationships, and overall well-being.

In addition to substance abuse, mental health challenges were also prevalent among the group members. The intense pressures of their careers, combined with personal struggles, took a toll on their mental well-being. Depression, anxiety, and other mental health issues were common experiences faced by various members of The Temptations.

Paul Williams, in particular, battled depression and alcoholism, which significantly affected his ability to perform and maintain stability in his personal life. These challenges ultimately led to his departure from the group in 1971. Williams tragically passed away in 1973, highlighting the devastating consequences that mental health struggles can have.

Despite these personal struggles, The Temptations continued to create remarkable music and deliver captivating performances. Their resilience and determination allowed them to overcome their individual challenges, supporting one another through difficult times and finding strength in their shared passion for music.

In the face of personal struggles, The Temptations also sought support from professionals and loved ones, recognizing the importance of seeking help and taking steps towards healing and recovery. The group's dedication to their craft and their commitment to one another helped them navigate the turbulent waters of their personal battles, finding solace in the music they created together. The Temptations' experiences with substance abuse and mental health serve as a reminder of the complexities that can accompany fame and success. Their stories highlight the importance of prioritizing mental health, seeking help when needed, and fostering a supportive environment within the music industry and beyond.

Despite the personal challenges they faced, The Temptations' music continued to resonate with audiences worldwide, serving as a testament to their resilience and enduring talent. Their ability to create soul-stirring music while confronting personal struggles is a testament to their strength and artistic integrity.

As The Temptations' journey continued, they would face further trials and triumphs, ultimately leaving an indelible mark on the history of popular music while inspiring others to persevere through personal struggles and find solace in the power of music.

Chapter 27: The Temptations' Legacy: Impact on R&B and Pop Music.

The Temptations' legacy in the realm of R&B and pop music is nothing short of extraordinary. Throughout their career, the group not only produced timeless hits and mesmerizing performances but also left an indelible impact on the genre and influenced countless artists who followed in their footsteps. This chapter explores the lasting legacy of The Temptations and their profound influence on the music world.

The Temptations' unique sound, characterized by their flawless harmonies, soulful delivery, and captivating stage presence, set a new standard for R&B and pop music. Their ability to seamlessly blend different genres, such as soul, funk, and disco, created a signature sound that was unmistakably their own. Their songs were marked by powerful storytelling, emotional depth, and social commentary, resonating with audiences of all backgrounds.

One of The Temptations' greatest contributions to the music world was their impeccable vocal harmonies. The group's ability to seamlessly blend their voices into a seamless tapestry of sound set them apart from their contemporaries. Their intricate vocal arrangements and meticulous attention to detail created a rich and dynamic sonic landscape that continues to inspire and influence artists to this day.

Furthermore, The Temptations' electrifying stage performances set a new benchmark for live shows. With their synchronized choreography, sharp suits, and polished routines, they captivated audiences with their energy and charisma. Their live performances were a true spectacle, leaving audiences in awe and setting the standard for future generations of performers.

The group's impact on R&B and pop music extended beyond their own era. The Temptations served as a source of inspiration for numerous artists who followed in their footsteps. Their influence can be heard in the work of artists such as Boyz II Men, The Backstreet Boys, and *NSYNC, who have all credited The Temptations as a major influence on their vocal stylings and showmanship.

In addition to their musical contributions, The Temptations played a significant role in breaking down racial barriers within the music industry. As one of the first African American groups to achieve mainstream success and recognition, they paved the way for future generations of Black artists. Their success not only opened doors for others but also challenged societal norms and helped shape a more inclusive and diverse music industry.

The Temptations' chart-topping hits, including classics like "My Girl," "Papa Was a Rollin' Stone," and "Ain't Too Proud to Beg," have become timeless anthems that continue to resonate with audiences of all ages. Their songs have been covered by countless artists and featured in films, commercials, and television shows, cementing their place in the fabric of popular culture.

Moreover, The Temptations' enduring popularity is evident in their numerous accolades and inductions into prestigious institutions. They have been inducted into the Rock and Roll Hall of Fame, the Vocal Group Hall of Fame, and the Rhythm and Blues Music Hall of Fame, among others. Their impact on the music industry has been recognized and celebrated by their peers and critics alike.

The Temptations' legacy continues to shine brightly, their music continuing to be celebrated and cherished by fans old and new. Their influence on R&B and pop music is immeasurable, with their innovative sound, impeccable harmonies, and dynamic performances leaving an indelible mark on the genre. The Temptations' legacy serves as a testament to their unparalleled talent, creativity, and enduring appeal.

As time goes on, The Temptations' music will undoubtedly continue to inspire generations of artists and continue to be celebrated as a cornerstone of R&B and pop music history. Their timeless hits and legendary performances ensure that The Temptations will forever be remembered as one of the greatest groups in music history, leaving an enduring legacy that will be cherished for generations to come.

Chapter 28: The 1980s: Staying Relevant in a Changing Industry

As the 1980s rolled in, the music industry underwent significant transformations, marked by the rise of new genres and changing tastes. The Temptations, a group with a rich history and an established sound, faced the challenge of staying relevant in this ever-changing landscape. This chapter explores how The Temptations navigated the 1980s, adapting their style while maintaining their core identity.

The 1980s brought forth a wave of new musical genres, such as pop, rock, and electronic music, that captured the attention of mainstream audiences. The Temptations, known for their soulful

R&B sound, understood the need to adapt their music to appeal to a broader audience without compromising their core identity.

In 1980, The Temptations released the album "Power," which showcased their willingness to embrace contemporary sounds and production techniques. The album featured a blend of R&B, funk, and disco influences, with tracks like "Power" and "Struck By Lightning" incorporating a more upbeat and energetic sound. This album demonstrated their commitment to staying relevant while maintaining their distinct vocal harmonies and soulful delivery.

The group's ability to collaborate with a diverse range of producers and songwriters was key to their success in the 1980s. They worked with esteemed producers like Thom Bell, Richard Perry, and Norman Whitfield, who helped them craft a sound that blended their classic style with contemporary elements. This strategic collaboration allowed The Temptations to appeal to both loyal fans and new listeners, ensuring their continued relevance in the changing musical landscape.

The 1980s also saw The Temptations release a string of successful singles. In 1983, they achieved a major comeback with the release of "Reunion," a collaboration with Rick James. The song became a chart-topping hit and reintroduced The Temptations to a new generation of music lovers. This success was followed by the release of the album "Surface Thrills" in 1983, which spawned the hits "Treat Her Like a Lady" and "My Love is True (Truly for You)." The group's ability to adapt their image and style was also evident in their stage performances. They incorporated modern dance moves and stylish attire, while still retaining their signature synchronized choreography. The Temptations embraced the visual aesthetics of the era while staying true to their roots, captivating audiences with their electrifying performances.

However, the 1980s also brought challenges for The Temptations. They experienced lineup changes, with members departing and new members joining the group. These transitions required the group to adjust and rebuild their dynamic, but they remained committed to their shared vision and the preservation of The Temptations' legacy.

While the 1980s presented both opportunities and obstacles, The Temptations demonstrated their resilience and adaptability. They managed to maintain their relevance through a combination of embracing contemporary sounds, collaborating with new producers, and delivering captivating performances that captivated audiences. Their ability to stay true to their core identity while incorporating new elements into their music ensured that The Temptations remained a relevant and respected force in the industry. Their willingness to evolve with the times without sacrificing their artistry is a testament to their enduring appeal and the enduring legacy they have built.

As the 1980s came to a close, The Temptations had proven that they could adapt to the changing music industry without compromising the essence of their sound. They continued to inspire and influence new generations of artists, leaving an indelible mark on R&B and pop music that would continue to resonate for years to come.

The Temptations' ability to navigate the challenges of the 1980s and stay relevant in a changing industry serves as a testament to their artistry, versatility, and dedication to their craft. Their enduring presence in the music world showcases their status as true legends and reinforces their place as one of the most iconic groups in the history of popular music.

Chapter 29: Collaborations and Crossover Success

Collaborations and crossover success played a significant role in The Temptations' journey, allowing them to expand their reach, explore new musical territories, and captivate audiences across genres. This chapter explores the group's notable collaborations and their ventures into different genres, cementing their status as versatile artists and contributing to their enduring legacy.

Throughout their career, The Temptations collaborated with a wide array of artists, crossing boundaries and genres to create memorable and groundbreaking music. These collaborations not only showcased the group's versatility but also allowed them to reach new audiences and further solidify their place in the music industry.

One of the most notable collaborations in The Temptations' discography was their work with legendary songwriter and producer Norman Whitfield. Together, they crafted numerous chart-topping hits, including the iconic "Papa Was a Rollin' Stone," which became a defining song for both The Temptations and the era. Whitfield's innovative production techniques, combined with

The Temptations' soulful vocals, resulted in a sound that was both groundbreaking and timeless.

The Temptations also collaborated with other renowned artists of their time, showcasing their ability to seamlessly blend their style with various musical sensibilities. Their collaboration with Diana Ross and the Supremes on the album "Diana Ross & the Supremes Join The Temptations" yielded hit songs such as "I'm Gonna Make You Love Me" and "I Second That Emotion." This crossover success bridged the gap between Motown's male and female vocal groups and solidified their collective impact on popular music.

Furthermore, The Temptations ventured into the realm of disco in the late 1970s, collaborating with producer Jeffrey Bowen on the album "A Song for You." This collaboration resulted in the hit single "Heavenly" and showcased the group's ability to adapt their sound to different genres, tapping into the disco era's pulsating rhythms and infectious melodies.

The group's collaborations extended beyond their Motown labelmates. In 1986, The Temptations joined forces with Hall & Oates for the single "The Way You Do the Things You Do," which not only brought their classic sound to a new generation but also introduced them to a wider pop audience. This collaboration demonstrated their ability to transcend genres and collaborate with artists from different musical backgrounds.

The Temptations' crossover success was not limited to collaborations. They ventured into the world of pop and adult contemporary music, reaching a broader audience and further solidifying their status as iconic performers. Songs like "Treat Her Like a Lady," "My Girl," and "Just My

Imagination (Running Away with Me)" crossed over to mainstream pop charts, showcasing the group's universal appeal and ability to transcend genre boundaries.

The group's ability to seamlessly blend their soulful R&B sound with other genres, collaborate with a diverse range of artists, and cross over into pop and adult contemporary charts is a testament to their musical versatility and timeless appeal. These collaborations and crossover ventures not only expanded their fan base but also solidified their place as one of the most influential and revered groups in popular music.

The Temptations' ability to adapt, collaborate, and successfully crossover into different genres allowed them to maintain relevance and captivate audiences across generations. Their artistry and willingness to explore new musical territories are a testament to their enduring legacy, inspiring future artists to push boundaries and create music that transcends traditional genres.

As The Temptations continued to navigate the ever-evolving music industry, their collaborations and crossover successes served as a testament to their versatility, creativity, and ability to connect with audiences on a universal level. Their contributions to the world of music extend far beyond their soulful R&B roots, solidifying their place in history as true icons of crossover success.

Chapter 30: Return to the Charts: "Treat Her Like a Lady"

In the mid-1980s, The Temptations experienced a remarkable resurgence on the music charts with the release of their hit single "Treat Her Like a Lady." This chapter delves into the story behind the song's creation, its impact on the group's career, and its enduring legacy as a testament to The Temptations' timeless appeal.

"Treat Her Like a Lady" was released in 1984 as part of The Temptations' album "Truly for You." Produced by Richard Perry and written by Otis Williams, Ali-Ollie Woodson, and Otis Williams' wife Josephine Armstead, the song carried a powerful message of respect and appreciation for women. Its infectious rhythm, memorable hooks, and soulful vocals made it an instant hit.

The song's success marked a pivotal moment for The Temptations. It not only marked their return to the top of the charts but also introduced them to a new generation of listeners. "Treat Her Like a Lady" reached the top of the R&B charts, becoming their first number-one hit in nearly a decade, and also made a significant impact on the pop charts, peaking at number three on the Billboard Hot 100. The song's popularity can be attributed to its universal appeal. Its message of treating women with respect and dignity resonated with audiences across genders and backgrounds. The powerful vocal performances, led by Ali-Ollie Woodson's soulful delivery, added an extra layer of emotion to the lyrics, creating an anthem that struck a chord with listeners.

"Treat Her Like a Lady" showcased The Temptations' ability to evolve with the times while staying true to their core identity. The song incorporated elements of contemporary R&B, pop, and dance music, capturing the spirit of the 1980s while maintaining the group's signature harmonies and soulful sound. This seamless blend of old and new elements contributed to the song's widespread appeal and its success on the charts.

The impact of "Treat Her Like a Lady" extended beyond its initial release. The song has become one of The Temptations' signature tunes, frequently performed in their live shows and remaining a fan favorite. Its enduring popularity is a testament to its timeless message and the group's ability to create music that resonates across generations.

Moreover, "Treat Her Like a Lady" solidified The Temptations' position as one of the most influential and enduring groups in the history of R&B and soul music. The song's success revitalized their career and paved the way for future achievements, opening doors for further chart success and critical acclaim.

The legacy of "Treat Her Like a Lady" continues to thrive today. The song's empowering message of love, respect, and equality remains relevant, serving as a reminder of the enduring power of The Temptations' music. It stands as a testament to their ability to create music that not only entertains but also uplifts and inspires.

In conclusion, "Treat Her Like a Lady" marked a triumphant return to the charts for The Temptations, reaffirming their status as one of the greatest groups in the history of popular music. The song's universal message, combined with the group's exceptional vocal performances, propelled it to chart success and solidified its place as an iconic hit in The Temptations' discography. "Treat Her Like a Lady" remains a timeless classic, exemplifying the enduring legacy and timeless appeal of The Temptations.

Chapter 31: Legacy and Longevity: The Temptations in the 1990s

As the 1990s dawned, The Temptations entered a new decade with an illustrious history and an enduring legacy. This chapter explores the group's journey in the 1990s, highlighting their continued success, contributions to the music industry, and their ability to maintain their status as one of the most influential and revered groups in popular music.

Despite having been in the music industry for several decades, The Temptations showed no signs of slowing down in the 1990s. They continued to release new music, tour extensively, and captivate audiences with their timeless sound and dynamic performances. Their ability to adapt to changing times while staying true to their roots contributed to their longevity and enduring appeal. In 1991, The Temptations released the album "Milestones," which showcased their ability to embrace contemporary R&B sounds while maintaining their signature harmonies and soulful delivery. The album featured the hit single "My Love," which reached the top of the R&B charts and demonstrated that The Temptations could still create music that resonated with audiences. Throughout the 1990s, The Temptations remained a popular live act, performing to enthusiastic audiences around the world. Their stage shows continued to captivate with their impeccable harmonies, intricate choreography, and energetic performances. The group's ability to connect with audiences through their live performances was a testament to their showmanship and the timeless quality of their music.

In addition to their live performances, The Temptations received numerous accolades and honors in the 1990s. They were inducted into the Rock and Roll Hall of Fame in 1989, solidifying their status as one of the most influential groups in the history of popular music. They also received the Grammy Lifetime Achievement Award in 2013, further recognizing their contributions to the music industry.

The group also continued to collaborate with other artists in the 1990s, further expanding their musical reach and influence. They worked with contemporary R&B artists such as Rick James, Teddy Pendergrass, and Luther Vandross, creating memorable collaborations that bridged the gap between generations and showcased the enduring appeal of The Temptations' sound.

In 1998, tragedy struck when founding member Melvin Franklin passed away. His death marked the end of an era but served as a reminder of the indelible impact The Temptations had made as a group. The loss of Franklin was deeply felt, but the remaining members were determined to carry on his legacy and the legacy of The Temptations.

As the 1990s came to a close, The Temptations had solidified their status as one of the most beloved and respected groups in the history of popular music. Their ability to adapt, evolve, and maintain their signature sound throughout the decades was a testament to their artistry and talent. They left an indelible mark on the music industry, influencing countless artists and continuing to inspire future generations.

The Temptations' legacy and longevity in the 1990s showcased their enduring appeal and the timeless quality of their music. Their ability to navigate changing musical landscapes while staying true to their core sound ensured their continued relevance and the admiration of fans worldwide. They proved that their music was not confined to a specific era but had the power to transcend time and touch the hearts of people across generations.

In conclusion, the 1990s marked another chapter in The Temptations' storied career, characterized by their continued success, electrifying performances, and the preservation of their enduring legacy. The group's ability to adapt, collaborate, and maintain their status as icons of soul music solidified their place in the annals of music history and ensured that The Temptations' influence would continue to be felt for years to come.

Chapter 32: Transition to New Generations: Changes in Lineup

Throughout their storied career, The Temptations experienced numerous lineup changes as members departed and new talents joined the group. This chapter explores the transitional period of The Temptations as they welcomed new members and navigated the challenges of maintaining their legacy while adapting to the demands of a changing music industry.

In the late 1990s and early 2000s, The Temptations underwent a significant transition in their lineup. Founding member Otis Williams remained a constant presence, providing stability and guidance during this period of change. However, several long-standing members, including David Ruffin, Eddie Kendricks, and Melvin Franklin, had left the group, leaving behind a rich musical legacy that would be hard to match.

To fill the void left by the departing members, The Temptations recruited new talents who would contribute their own unique voices and styles to the group. Among the notable additions were Ali-Ollie Woodson, Theo Peoples, and Ron Tyson. These talented vocalists brought their own flair and artistry to the group, injecting new energy and revitalizing The Temptations' sound.

Ali-Ollie Woodson, who had previously collaborated with the group in the 1980s, rejoined The Temptations in 1984 and became an integral part of their lineup during the transitional period. His powerful and soulful voice added a contemporary edge to the group's sound, helping them stay relevant in an ever-changing music landscape.

Theo Peoples, a seasoned R&B vocalist, joined The Temptations in 1992, bringing his smooth and versatile voice to the group. His addition to the lineup showcased The Temptations' commitment to finding talented singers who could carry on the group's legacy while adding their own personal touch.

Ron Tyson, another accomplished vocalist, joined The Temptations in 1983 and has remained with the group to this day. His soaring tenor and charismatic stage presence have made him a vital part of The Temptations' performances and recordings, adding a fresh dimension to their sound.

The transition to new generations within The Temptations was not without its challenges. The departure of beloved members inevitably led to comparisons and raised expectations from both fans and critics. However, the new lineup members demonstrated their talent and commitment, earning the respect and admiration of audiences worldwide. The Temptations continued to release new music throughout this transitional period, proving that they were not content to rest on their laurels. They explored contemporary R&B sounds while staying true to their iconic harmonies and soulful roots. Albums such as "Phoenix Rising" (1998) and "Awesome" (2001) showcased the group's ability to adapt to changing musical trends without compromising their signature sound.

The new lineup's contributions breathed new life into The Temptations, allowing them to connect with younger audiences while maintaining their loyal fan base. The group's live performances remained a highlight, featuring their classic hits alongside new material. The collective talent and chemistry of the new members ensured that The Temptations' legacy would continue to thrive.

While the lineup changes marked a significant transition for The Temptations, they also served as a testament to the group's resilience and enduring legacy. The ability to attract new talent and evolve with the times while staying true to their musical roots contributed to their longevity and continued relevance.

In conclusion, the transition to new generations within The Temptations marked a period of change and adaptation for the group. Through the recruitment of talented vocalists and their dedication to creating new music, The Temptations proved that their legacy would endure and that their sound would continue to resonate with audiences of all ages. The new lineup members brought their own unique contributions, helping to maintain the group's iconic status while ushering in a new chapter in The Temptations' remarkable journey.

Chapter 33: The Temptations in the New Millennium

As the new millennium dawned, The Temptations embarked on a new chapter in their illustrious career. This chapter explores the group's journey in the 2000s and beyond, highlighting their continued dedication to their craft, their enduring popularity, and their unwavering commitment to their musical legacy.

The Temptations entered the new millennium with a lineup that included stalwart member Otis Williams, along with talented vocalists such as Ron Tyson, Terry Weeks, and Bruce Williamson. Together, they forged ahead, carrying on the group's iconic sound and captivating audiences around the world.

In the 2000s, The Temptations continued to tour extensively, bringing their electrifying performances to fans across the globe. Their live shows remained a testament to their showmanship, vocal prowess, and exceptional harmonies. Audiences were treated to a rich repertoire of classic hits as well as new material, showcasing the group's versatility and ability to connect with audiences old and new.

The Temptations also released new albums, demonstrating their ongoing creativity and commitment to evolving their sound. Albums such as "For Lovers Only" (2002) and "Reflections" (2005) showcased their ability to reinterpret timeless classics while infusing them with a contemporary flair. The group's dedication to recording new material reflected their desire to remain relevant in an ever-changing music industry.

In addition to their own projects, The Temptations collaborated with various artists and musicians, further solidifying their status as influential figures in the music industry. They joined forces with artists such as The Supremes, Diana Ross, and Smokey Robinson, creating memorable performances and reminding audiences of their enduring impact. Throughout the new millennium, The Temptations continued to receive accolades and recognition for their contributions to music. They were inducted into the Vocal Group Hall of Fame in 2001, the Grammy Hall of Fame in 2002, and received the Grammy Lifetime Achievement Award in 2013. These honors further affirmed their status as true icons of popular music.

Tragically, the group faced the loss of several beloved members in the new millennium. In 2003, Ali-Ollie Woodson, who had made a significant impact during his tenure with The Temptations, passed away. His soulful vocals and dynamic stage presence had made a lasting impression on both the group and their fans.

Despite the challenges and the loss of cherished members, The Temptations pressed on, proving their resilience and commitment to their craft. New talents were welcomed into the group, ensuring a seamless transition and keeping the spirit of The Temptations alive.

As the years rolled on, The Temptations continued to inspire generations of artists and music lovers alike. Their timeless sound and impeccable performances attracted audiences of all ages, bridging the gap between the past and the present. Their influence could be heard in the works of contemporary artists who were inspired by their harmonies, style, and showmanship.

In conclusion, The Temptations' journey in the new millennium showcased their enduring popularity, unwavering commitment to their musical legacy, and their ability to captivate audiences across generations. As they navigated the ever-changing music industry, they remained true to their core sound while embracing new influences and collaborations. The Temptations' music and performances continued to resonate with fans worldwide, ensuring that their legacy would live on for years to come.

Chapter 34: Otis Williams: The Last Original Member

Throughout the rich history of The Temptations, one constant figure has remained at the center of the group's success and longevity: Otis Williams. As the last original member standing, Otis Williams has played a pivotal role in shaping the group's legacy, preserving their sound, and carrying the torch of The Temptations into the present day.

Otis Williams was born on October 30, 1941, in Texarkana, Texas. He moved to Detroit, Michigan, during his childhood, where he would eventually become a key figure in the city's vibrant music scene. As a young man, Williams was drawn to the harmonies and rhythms of vocal groups, and he aspired to make a name for himself in the music industry.

In 1960, Williams co-founded The Temptations alongside Elbridge "Al" Bryant, Melvin Franklin, Eddie Kendricks, and Paul Williams. From their early days, Otis Williams emerged as the group's anchor, providing stability, leadership, and a strong vision for their future. His deep baritone voice and charismatic stage presence became a vital component of The Temptations' sound.

Over the decades, as various members came and went, Otis Williams remained a constant presence and the driving force behind The Temptations' success. His dedication to the group and unwavering commitment to their musical legacy helped steer The Temptations through various challenges and transitions.

As the last original member, Otis Williams took on the responsibility of preserving The Temptations' unique sound and ensuring that the group's performances remained true to their roots. His deep understanding of the group's history and his ability to adapt to changing times enabled The Temptations to remain relevant and captivating to audiences of all ages.

Throughout his career, Otis Williams has been not only a talented vocalist but also a skilled collaborator and producer. He played an instrumental role in shaping The Temptations' signature harmonies, working closely with the other members to create their distinctive sound. Additionally, he collaborated with renowned songwriters and producers, contributing to the group's extensive repertoire of timeless hits.

Otis Williams' leadership and dedication to The Temptations have been widely recognized and honored. In 1989, the group was inducted into the Rock and Roll Hall of Fame, a testament to their enduring impact on popular music. Williams, as the last original member, accepted the honor on behalf of the group, acknowledging the collective achievements and contributions of all the members who had passed through the ranks.

Despite the passage of time and the changes in the music industry, Otis Williams has remained steadfast in his commitment to The Temptations. His passion for the music, his loyalty to the group's legacy, and his unwavering determination to carry on their tradition have earned him the respect and admiration of fans and fellow musicians alike.

In recent years, as The Temptations continue to perform and captivate audiences, Otis Williams' presence on stage serves as a poignant reminder of the group's enduring legacy. His voice, still resonant and powerful, embodies the spirit of The Temptations, carrying forward the rich musical heritage that has touched the hearts of millions around the world.

In conclusion, Otis Williams stands as a pillar of strength and a living link to The Temptations' storied past. As the last original member, he has guided the group through triumphs and tribulations, preserving their sound and ensuring that their music continues to inspire and uplift. Otis Williams' contributions to The Temptations' legacy are immeasurable, and his enduring presence serves as a testament to the timeless quality of their music.

Chapter 35: The Supporting Cast: Appreciating the Contributions

While The Temptations have rightfully garnered attention for their incredible vocal harmonies, charismatic performances, and enduring hits, it is essential to recognize the contributions of the supporting cast members who played integral roles in the group's success. This chapter pays tribute to the talented individuals who supported The Temptations behind the scenes, including musicians, songwriters, producers, and the dedicated team at Motown Records.

The Temptations' success was not solely dependent on their vocal abilities but also on the exceptional musicians who provided the instrumental backdrop for their performances and recordings. The backing band, often referred to as the Funk Brothers, played a crucial role in creating the signature Motown sound that defined The Temptations' music. These talented session musicians, including guitarists, bassists, drummers, and keyboardists, brought their expertise and creativity to the table, contributing to the overall sonic richness of the group's recordings.

In addition to the musicians, the songwriters and producers associated with The Temptations deserve recognition for their invaluable contributions. Motown Records, under the leadership of Berry Gordy, Jr., fostered an environment that nurtured and showcased talented songwriters and producers. Figures such as Smokey Robinson, Norman Whitfield, and Holland-Dozier-Holland played instrumental roles in crafting the group's hits and developing their unique sound.

Smokey Robinson, a gifted songwriter and producer, wrote several of The Temptations' early hits, including "The Way You Do the Things You Do" and "My Girl." His soulful compositions perfectly complemented the group's vocal abilities and helped establish their place in the hearts of fans worldwide.

Norman Whitfield, another prolific songwriter and producer, took The Temptations' sound in a bold new direction during the late 1960s and early 1970s. Collaborating with Barrett Strong, he penned hits like "Ain't Too Proud to Beg" and "Papa Was a Rollin' Stone." Whitfield's innovative production techniques and socially conscious lyrics added depth and relevance to The Temptations' music, further solidifying their status as trailblazers. The songwriting and production team of Holland-Dozier-Holland, consisting of Brian Holland, Lamont Dozier, and Eddie Holland, also made significant contributions to The Temptations' success. Their catchy and infectious compositions, such as "I Can't Help Myself (Sugar Pie Honey Bunch)" and "Get Ready," showcased The Temptations' versatility and ability to deliver both heartfelt ballads and energetic dance tracks. Beyond the musicians, songwriters, and producers, The Temptations' success relied on the support and guidance of the Motown Records family. Berry Gordy, Jr., the founder of Motown, recognized the immense talent of The Temptations and provided the platform and resources necessary for their growth. His vision and business acumen propelled the group to international acclaim and helped shape their trajectory in the music industry. Additionally, the Motown Records team, including managers, agents, and marketing professionals, played crucial roles in promoting The Temptations' music, coordinating their tours, and ensuring their success. Their collective efforts and unwavering dedication contributed to the group's rise to prominence and sustained their popularity over the years.

In conclusion, The Temptations' success was a collective effort, and it is essential to appreciate the contributions of the supporting cast who played vital roles behind the scenes. The talented musicians, songwriters, producers, and the dedicated team at

Motown Records all played integral parts in shaping the group's sound, guiding their career, and ensuring their place in music history. The collaboration and synergy between these individuals resulted in the timeless music that continues to captivate audiences and defines The Temptations' legacy.

Chapter 36: David Ruffin's Legacy: Life and Tragic End

David Ruffin, with his mesmerizing voice and dynamic stage presence, left an indelible mark on the legacy of The Temptations. This chapter explores the life and tragic end of David Ruffin, shedding light on his immense talent, personal struggles, and lasting impact on the world of music. David Ruffin was born on January 18, 1941, in Whynot, Mississippi. Raised in a musical family, he developed a passion for singing at a young age. In 1964, Ruffin joined The Temptations as the group's new lead vocalist, replacing Elbridge "Al" Bryant.

His distinctive voice, characterized by its gritty and soulful quality, added a new dimension to the group's sound.

Ruffin's tenure with The Temptations marked a period of unparalleled success and artistic growth. His powerful vocals and charismatic stage presence helped propel the group to new heights, earning them numerous chart-topping hits and a devoted fan base. Songs like "My Girl," "Ain't Too Proud to Beg," and "I Wish It Would Rain" showcased Ruffin's emotional range and contributed to The Temptations' status as one of the premier vocal groups of their time.

Despite his professional achievements, Ruffin faced personal struggles that would eventually take a toll on his life and career. He battled addiction and had a tumultuous relationship with fellow group members and management. His behavior became increasingly erratic, leading to conflicts within the group and strained relationships.

In 1968, Ruffin's solo career began with the release of his album "My Whole World Ended." The title track became a hit, and Ruffin embarked on a solo career alongside his continued work with The Temptations. His solo endeavors showcased his raw talent and versatility as a performer, but they were also marred by his personal demons, including drug addiction and legal troubles.

Tragically, David Ruffin's life was cut short on June 1, 1991, when he passed away at the age of 50. His death was attributed to a drug overdose, marking a devastating end to a talented artist who had left an indelible impact on the world of music.

Despite the circumstances surrounding his death, David Ruffin's legacy as a soul icon and his contributions to The Temptations endure. His distinct voice, impassioned delivery, and magnetic stage presence continue to captivate audiences to this day. Ruffin's influence can be heard in the works of countless artists who have been inspired by his vocal style and emotive performances.

Beyond his music, David Ruffin's tragic end serves as a poignant reminder of the challenges faced by many artists in the industry. His struggles with addiction and personal demons highlight the importance of mental health and the need for support and understanding within the music community.

In conclusion, David Ruffin's legacy is one of incredible talent, unforgettable performances, and personal struggles. His time with The Temptations and his subsequent solo career left an indelible mark on the world of soul music. Though his life was cut short, his impact continues to resonate, and his music remains a testament to his immense talent and the enduring legacy of The Temptations.

Chapter 37: Paul Williams' Legacy: Contributions and Tragedy

Paul Williams, a founding member of The Temptations, made significant contributions to the group's success with his soulful voice, charismatic presence, and choreography skills. This chapter delves into Paul Williams' legacy, his invaluable contributions to The Temptations' sound and image, and the tragic circumstances that overshadowed his life.

Born on July 2, 1939, in Birmingham, Alabama, Paul Williams moved to Detroit, Michigan, during his early years. In 1960, alongside Otis Williams, Melvin Franklin, Eddie Kendricks, and Elbridge "Al" Bryant, he formed The Temptations. Paul Williams' smooth tenor voice and captivating stage presence quickly became a distinguishing feature of the group's performances.

Beyond his vocal abilities, Paul Williams played a crucial role in developing The Temptations' choreography. He showcased his natural talent for dance, adding a dynamic visual element to their stage shows. Williams' innovative dance moves and synchronized routines became a signature of The Temptations' performances, setting them apart from other vocal groups of the time.

During the 1960s, Paul Williams' voice and stage presence were prominently featured in many of The Temptations' hit songs. He delivered memorable performances on tracks like "The Way You Do the

Things You Do," "Just My Imagination (Running Away with Me)," and "I Wish It Would Rain." Williams' ability to convey deep emotion and vulnerability through his vocals contributed to the group's success and endeared them to fans around the world.

However, behind the scenes, Paul Williams faced personal struggles that would ultimately overshadow his legacy. He battled with alcoholism and other health issues, which affected his ability to perform and impacted his overall well-being. Williams' declining health and increasing dependency on alcohol strained his relationships within the group and impacted his professional contributions.

Tragically, Paul Williams' life was cut short on August 17, 1973, when he died from an apparent self-inflicted gunshot wound. His death was ruled a suicide, marking a heartbreaking end to a talented artist who had made significant contributions to The Temptations' success.

Despite the tragic circumstances surrounding his death, Paul Williams' legacy lives on through his artistic contributions to The Temptations. His soulful voice, captivating stage presence, and innovative choreography continue to inspire artists in the realms of soul, R&B, and pop music. Williams' impact on the group's image and live performances cannot be overstated, as his contributions helped shape The Temptations' identity and set them apart as a groundbreaking vocal group.

In recognition of his influence and contributions, Paul Williams was posthumously inducted into the Rock and Roll Hall of Fame as a member of The Temptations in 1989. This honor acknowledges his role in shaping the group's success and acknowledges his enduring impact on the world of music.

In conclusion, Paul Williams' legacy is one of immense talent, stage presence, and creative contributions to The Temptations' sound and image. Despite the personal struggles he faced, his impact on the group's success and his influential role in the world of soul music cannot be understated. Paul Williams' tragic end serves as a reminder of the importance of mental health and the challenges faced by artists in the pursuit of their craft. His contributions and artistry continue to resonate, ensuring his lasting legacy within the music industry.

Chapter 38: Melvin Franklin's Legacy: The Deep Bass Voice

Melvin Franklin, known for his deep bass voice and powerful vocal presence, played an integral role in defining the sound and success of The Temptations. In this chapter, we explore Melvin Franklin's legacy, his unmatched vocal abilities, and the lasting impact he made as a member of one of the most iconic vocal groups in music history.

Born David Melvin English on October 12, 1942, in Montgomery, Alabama, Melvin Franklin showcased his exceptional vocal range from a young age. His deep bass voice, resonant and velvety, possessed a unique richness that added depth and texture to The Temptations' harmonies. Franklin's voice became a defining element of the group's sound, setting them apart from their contemporaries.

Joining The Temptations in 1960 as a founding member, Melvin Franklin provided the foundation for the group's harmonies. His deep bass vocals served as the anchor, supporting and complementing the higher tenor voices of his fellow group members. Franklin's remarkable vocal control and ability to effortlessly hit low notes added a layer of richness and complexity to The Temptations' music.

Throughout the 1960s and 1970s, Melvin Franklin's distinctive voice featured prominently on many of The Temptations' chart-topping hits. Songs like "My Girl," "Ain't Too Proud to Beg," and "Papa Was a Rollin' Stone" showcased Franklin's deep, resonant tones, captivating listeners and solidifying The Temptations' status as soul music icons.

Beyond his vocal abilities, Melvin Franklin brought a calm and composed presence to the group. Often referred to as "The Preacher" due to his authoritative and spiritual aura, Franklin's stage presence exuded confidence and added a sense of gravitas to The Temptations' performances. His smooth dance moves and commanding stage demeanor captivated audiences and further enhanced the group's visual appeal.

Melvin Franklin's contributions to The Temptations extended beyond his vocal prowess. He played a vital role in maintaining the group's harmonies during live performances, ensuring that their signature sound remained intact. Franklin's ability to blend his deep bass tones with the other members' voices created a seamless and unified vocal blend that became a trademark of The Temptations' sound.

Tragically, Melvin Franklin's life was cut short on February 23, 1995, when he passed away at the age of 52 due to complications from a brain seizure. His death marked a profound loss for the music industry and left a void that could never be filled. Franklin's unmatched deep bass voice and his presence as a member of The Temptations were irreplaceable.

Melvin Franklin's legacy as a soul music icon and his contributions to The Temptations' success continue to resonate today. His distinctive vocal style and stage presence set a standard for deep bass voices in popular music. Many artists have been inspired by his talent, attempting to capture the same depth and resonance that made Franklin's voice so iconic.

In recognition of his contributions, Melvin Franklin was posthumously inducted into the Rock and Roll Hall of Fame as a member of The Temptations in 1989. This honor reflects the profound impact he made as a member of one of the greatest vocal groups of all time.

In conclusion, Melvin Franklin's legacy as the deep bass voice of The Temptations is one of immense talent, unmatched vocal abilities, and unwavering presence. His resonant tones and commanding stage presence helped shape The Temptations' sound and solidify their place in music history. Melvin Franklin's contributions to soul music endure, and his legacy as a soulful and influential vocalist remains unparalleled.

Chapter 39: Grammy Recognition: Awards and Nominations

The Temptations' impact on the music industry was not only felt by audiences and fans but also recognized by prestigious award organizations. This chapter explores The Temptations' Grammy recognition, highlighting their awards and nominations, and acknowledging their enduring influence on the world of music.

Throughout their illustrious career, The Temptations received multiple Grammy nominations and were honored with several prestigious awards. Their unique blend of soulful harmonies, captivating performances, and timeless songs garnered critical acclaim and solidified their status as one of the most influential vocal groups in history.

The first Grammy recognition for The Temptations came in 1965 when their signature hit "My Girl" received a nomination for Best Rhythm & Blues Recording. Although they didn't win that year, it was a testament to the group's growing popularity and the undeniable appeal of their music.

The following year, in 1966, The Temptations were nominated once again in the same category for their hit single "Ain't Too Proud to Beg." This nomination further cemented their place among the top performers in the R&B genre.

In 1969, The Temptations achieved a significant milestone when they won their first Grammy Award. Their iconic song "Cloud Nine" took home the award for Best Rhythm & Blues Performance by a Duo or Group. This win was a momentous occasion, as it not only recognized the group's talent but also acknowledged the groundbreaking fusion of soul and psychedelic influences in their music.

The success continued for The Temptations, earning them additional Grammy nominations in subsequent years. In 1972, their single "Just My Imagination (Running Away with Me)" received a nomination for Best Rhythm & Blues Performance by a Duo or Group. This timeless ballad showcased the group's ability to deliver poignant and emotionally resonant performances.

One of The Temptations' most celebrated songs, "Papa Was a Rollin' Stone," brought them further Grammy recognition. Released in 1972, the song earned nominations for both Record of the Year and Best Rhythm & Blues Performance by a Duo or Group with Vocals. The song's epic arrangement, powerful vocals, and social commentary solidified its place as a classic in the music world.

Although The Temptations' Grammy wins were limited, their influence and impact on the music industry cannot be understated. Their nomination and recognition by the Recording Academy reflect their significant contributions to the R&B and soul genres and their enduring legacy.

Beyond their specific Grammy nominations and wins, The Temptations' body of work continues to receive accolades and be celebrated by fans and critics alike. Their songs are frequently featured on lists of the greatest hits of all time, and their contributions to popular music are often cited as influential and groundbreaking.

In conclusion, The Temptations' Grammy recognition serves as a testament to their exceptional talent, groundbreaking sound, and lasting impact on the music industry. While their wins were modest in number, their nominations and critical acclaim solidify their place among the greatest vocal groups of all time. The enduring popularity of their music and their continued influence on subsequent generations of artists demonstrate the timeless appeal and significance of The Temptations' contributions to the world of music.

Chapter 40: Induction into the Rock and Roll Hall of Fame

The Temptations' enduring impact on the music industry was officially recognized with their induction into the Rock and Roll Hall of Fame. This chapter delves into the significance of this prestigious honor, highlighting The Temptations' induction and celebrating their influential contributions to rock and roll.

In 1989, The Temptations received the ultimate validation when they were inducted into the Rock and Roll Hall of Fame. This recognition solidified their status as one of the most influential and iconic groups in the history of popular music. The induction ceremony, held at the Waldorf-Astoria Hotel in New York City, was a momentous occasion that honored the group's remarkable achievements and celebrated their lasting impact on the genre. The Temptations' induction into the Rock and Roll Hall of Fame marked a milestone not only for the group but also for the genre of soul music. It acknowledged the group's unique blend of soulful harmonies, dynamic stage presence, and their ability to transcend musical boundaries. Their music resonated with audiences of all backgrounds and played a significant role in breaking down racial barriers in the music industry.

The induction ceremony served as a poignant reminder of The Temptations' influence on subsequent generations of artists. Their innovative vocal arrangements, choreography, and stylish image set new standards for performance and inspired countless musicians across various genres. The group's ability to seamlessly fuse soul,

R&B, and pop elements into their music showcased their versatility and helped shape the sound of popular music.

The Temptations' induction into the Rock and Roll Hall of Fame was also a testament to their longevity and sustained success. It recognized their ability to evolve and adapt to changing musical landscapes while remaining true to their unique sound and artistic vision. Their resilience and enduring popularity continue to inspire and influence artists to this day.

Beyond the individual members of the group, the induction into the Rock and Roll Hall of Fame recognized The Temptations as an institution and celebrated their collective contributions. It acknowledged the combined talents of the various members who had contributed to the group's success over the years, including those who had since departed or passed away. The honor solidified The Temptations' legacy as a groundbreaking and influential force in the world of music.

Induction into the Rock and Roll Hall of Fame is a distinction reserved for the most exceptional artists who have made a lasting impact on the rock and roll genre. The Temptations' induction serves as a testament to their talent, creativity, and significant contributions to popular music. It ensures their place among the legends of rock and roll and guarantees that their legacy will continue to be celebrated and revered for generations to come.

In conclusion, The Temptations' induction into the Rock and Roll Hall of Fame is a crowning achievement that recognizes their immense talent, cultural significance, and enduring legacy. It solidifies their place as one of the most influential vocal groups in the history of popular music and pays homage to their groundbreaking contributions to rock and roll. The honor serves as a testament to their lasting impact and ensures that The Temptations' music will continue to inspire and captivate audiences for years to come.

Chapter 41: The Temptations' Influence on Future Artists

The Temptations' impact on the music industry extends far beyond their chart-topping hits and legendary performances. Their innovative sound, soulful harmonies, and captivating stage presence have left an indelible mark on future generations of artists. This chapter explores The Temptations' profound influence on subsequent musicians and celebrates their enduring legacy.

One of the key aspects of The Temptations' influence is their unique vocal blend and harmonies. Their ability to seamlessly weave together different vocal parts, from the deep bass to the soaring tenor, created a distinct sound that became their signature. This approach to harmonization set a new standard for vocal groups and inspired countless artists to explore complex vocal arrangements and harmonies in their own music.

The Temptations' stage presence and choreography also had a profound impact on future artists. Their synchronized dance moves, smooth transitions, and captivating performances captivated audiences worldwide. Artists such as Michael Jackson, Usher, and Justin Timberlake have cited The Temptations as inspirations for their own stagecraft, incorporating elements of their showmanship into their performances.

Beyond their musicality and stage presence, The Temptations' lyrics often explored themes of love, social commentary, and personal struggles. Their songs addressed universal emotions and experiences, resonating with listeners across generations. Many artists have been influenced by The Temptations' ability to convey meaningful messages through their music, inspiring them to use their own lyrics as a platform for storytelling and reflection.

The influence of The Temptations can be heard in a wide range of musical genres. From R&B and soul to pop, rock, and even hip-hop, their impact transcends boundaries. Artists such as Boyz II Men, Destiny's Child, Bruno Mars, and John

Legend have all acknowledged The Temptations' influence on their own music and artistry. The Temptations' innovative sound and musical arrangements continue to inspire contemporary artists to push boundaries and explore new sonic territories. Their fusion of soul, R&B, and pop elements paved the way for future genres such as neo-soul and contemporary R&B. Their ability to evolve and adapt while staying true to their roots serves as a blueprint for artists seeking to carve their own path in the music industry.

Furthermore, The Temptations' success and longevity as a vocal group have set a standard for teamwork and collaboration. Their ability to maintain a harmonious dynamic within the group while showcasing the individual talents of each member has become a model for other vocal groups and bands. The chemistry and camaraderie displayed by The Temptations serve as a reminder of the power of unity and shared vision in creating timeless music.

In conclusion, The Temptations' influence on future artists cannot be overstated. Their innovative sound, soulful harmonies, captivating stage presence, and meaningful lyrics have left an indelible mark on the music industry. They have inspired countless artists to push creative boundaries, explore intricate vocal arrangements, and deliver powerful performances. The Temptations' enduring legacy serves as a testament to their artistry and their impact on shaping the sound and direction of popular music for generations to come.

Chapter 42: Breaking Barriers: The Temptations and Racial Integration.

The Temptations not only revolutionized the music industry with their innovative sound and captivating performances, but they also played a significant role in breaking down racial barriers during a time of segregation and racial tension in America. This chapter explores how The Temptations defied racial boundaries and became pioneers of racial integration in the music industry.

In the 1960s, when The Temptations rose to prominence, racial segregation was still deeply entrenched in American society. The music industry, like many other sectors, reflected this division, with separate charts and categories for black and white artists. However, The Temptations' music transcended racial boundaries and appealed to audiences of all backgrounds.

With their polished harmonies, dynamic stage presence, and undeniable talent, The Temptations captured the hearts of fans from diverse racial and cultural backgrounds. Their music united people through the power of soulful melodies and relatable lyrics that resonated with audiences regardless of their race.

The success of The Temptations challenged the prevailing norms of racial segregation in the music industry. Their popularity and cross-cultural appeal forced radio stations and concert venues to rethink their policies and open their doors to integrated audiences. The group's widespread recognition and acceptance demonstrated the unifying power of music and helped pave the way for greater racial integration in the industry.

Moreover, The Temptations' lineup itself represented racial integration. The group, originally formed with a mixture of African American and Mexican American members, showcased a diverse range of talent and backgrounds. This diversity within the group not only enhanced their musical sound but also served as a symbol of unity and inclusivity.

The Temptations' success was instrumental in breaking down barriers for future African American artists in the music industry. Their achievements helped dismantle stereotypes and paved the way for more opportunities and recognition for black musicians. By showcasing their immense talent and professionalism, The Temptations proved that talent knows no racial boundaries and that music can bridge divides.

The group's impact extended beyond the music industry. Their success and visibility as black artists who achieved mainstream success inspired hope and pride within the African American community. Their rise to stardom showed that barriers could be broken, dreams could be realized, and talent could triumph over prejudice.

The Temptations' influence on racial integration continues to reverberate in the music industry today. Their legacy serves as a reminder of the power of art to transcend societal divisions and promote unity. Their music brought people together, challenged stereotypes, and helped foster a more inclusive and equitable industry.

In conclusion, The Temptations played a pivotal role in breaking down racial barriers in the music industry. Through their music and performances, they united audiences of different racial backgrounds and challenged the prevailing norms of segregation. Their success and influence opened doors for future black artists and paved the way for greater racial integration in the music industry. The Temptations' impact on racial equality, alongside their unparalleled talent, ensures their place as not only musical legends but also as trailblazers in the fight for social justice and equality.

Chapter 43: The Temptations in Popular Culture: Movies and Television

The Temptations' impact extends beyond the realm of music. Their iconic status and captivating story have been immortalized in movies and television, further solidifying their place in popular culture. This chapter explores how The Temptations have been

portrayed on the screen, from biopics to television appearances, and how their story continues to captivate audiences across different mediums.
One of the most notable depictions of The Temptations in popular culture is the 1998 television miniseries titled "The Temptations." This miniseries, produced by the NBC network, chronicles the group's rise to fame, the challenges they faced, and their enduring musical legacy. The series received critical acclaim and introduced a new generation to the story of The Temptations, reaching a wide audience and reigniting interest in the group's music.
In addition to the miniseries, The Temptations' story has been adapted into a feature film. The 1998 movie "The Temptations," directed by Allan Arkush, delves into the highs and lows of the group's journey, capturing their struggles with fame,

personal conflicts, and triumphs. The film brings The Temptations' story to life on the big screen, showcasing their timeless music and the indelible mark they left on the music industry.

The influence of The Temptations can also be seen in various television appearances throughout the years. They made frequent appearances on popular TV shows of their time, including "The Ed Sullivan Show," "American Bandstand," and "Soul Train." These performances not only showcased their immense talent but also introduced their music to a wider audience, solidifying their status as beloved entertainers.

Beyond biopics and television appearances, The Temptations' music continues to be prominently featured in movies and television shows. Their classic hits have become synonymous with certain moments or evoke a specific era, adding depth and nostalgia to various storytelling mediums. Whether it's the iconic opening scene of "The Big Chill" set to "Ain't Too Proud to Beg" or the use of "My Girl" in films like "My Girl" itself and "Good Morning, Vietnam," The Temptations' songs have become woven into the fabric of popular culture.

Furthermore, The Temptations' influence can be seen in the work of contemporary artists who pay homage to the group through covers and samples of their songs. From artists like Boyz II Men and Christina Aguilera to Kanye West and Jay-Z, The Temptations' music has been reimagined and reinterpreted, breathing new life into their timeless classics and introducing their music to a new generation.

The enduring presence of The Temptations in popular culture is a testament to their lasting impact and universal appeal. Their story continues to resonate with audiences, inspiring filmmakers, and storytellers to explore their journey and celebrate their music. The Temptations' contributions to popular culture extend far beyond their time in the spotlight, ensuring that their legacy remains an integral part of the entertainment landscape.

In conclusion, The Temptations' influence in popular culture extends beyond their music. Their story has been brought to life through television miniseries and feature films, introducing their remarkable journey to new generations. Their music continues to be celebrated and referenced in movies and television shows, capturing the essence of different eras and evoking nostalgia. The Temptations' impact can be felt not only in their own performances but also in the work of contemporary artists who draw inspiration from their timeless sound. Their presence in popular culture ensures that The Temptations' legacy will endure for years to come.

Chapter 44: Continuing the Legacy: Tribute Acts and Revivals

The Temptations' timeless music and captivating performances have inspired a multitude of tribute acts and revivals, ensuring that their legacy lives on in the hearts of fans around the world. This chapter explores the ongoing influence of The Temptations through tribute acts, revivals, and the preservation of their iconic sound and stage presence.

Tribute acts dedicated to honoring The Temptations have emerged as a testament to the enduring popularity of the group's music. These talented performers strive to recreate the magic of The Temptations' live shows, capturing their distinctive harmonies, choreography, and charismatic stage presence. Through meticulous attention to detail and a deep appreciation for The Temptations' artistry, tribute acts pay homage to the group's timeless music and ensure that their spirit lives on.

Revivals of The Temptations' music have also played a significant role in keeping their legacy alive. Artists and bands continue to be inspired by The Temptations' sound and incorporate elements of their style into their own music. The influence of The Temptations can be heard in contemporary R&B and soul artists who carry on the tradition of smooth harmonies, infectious grooves, and heartfelt performances.

Beyond tribute acts and revivals, The Temptations' music continues to be celebrated through dedicated concerts, performances, and special events. These showcases not only pay homage to The Temptations' iconic catalog of songs but also introduce their music to new generations of listeners. The enduring appeal of The Temptations' music ensures that their songs remain relevant and cherished in the ever-evolving landscape of popular music.

The continued popularity of The Temptations' music is a testament to the timeless quality of their sound and the impact they had on the music industry. Their songs, such as "My Girl," "Papa Was a Rollin' Stone," and "Ain't Too Proud to Beg," remain beloved classics that resonate with audiences of all ages. The enduring popularity of these songs and the dedication of tribute acts and revivals serve as a testament to The Temptations' ongoing influence. Moreover, the preservation of The Temptations' legacy goes beyond tribute acts and revivals. Their music continues to be featured in movies, television shows, and commercials, exposing new audiences to their timeless sound. This exposure ensures that The Temptations' music reaches listeners who may not be familiar with their original recordings, further solidifying their place in popular culture.

In conclusion, tribute acts, revivals, and the ongoing celebration of The Temptations' music play a crucial role in continuing their legacy. These dedicated performers and events keep the spirit of The Temptations alive by recreating their distinctive sound and stage presence. The enduring popularity of The Temptations' music and their ongoing influence on contemporary artists serve as a testament to their impact on the music industry. As fans continue to enjoy the timeless melodies and soulful harmonies of The Temptations, their legacy remains firmly intact, ensuring that their music will continue to captivate audiences for generations to come.

Chapter 45: The Temptations' Enduring Popularity: Touring and Performances.

Despite the passage of time, The Temptations' enduring popularity has continued to captivate audiences worldwide. Their iconic music, electrifying performances, and timeless appeal have solidified their status as one of the most beloved and influential groups in the history of popular music. This chapter explores how The Temptations have maintained their relevance and connection with fans through extensive touring and live performances.

Touring has been a cornerstone of The Temptations' career, allowing them to share their music and stage presence with fans across the globe. The group's live performances have become legendary, known for their exceptional vocal harmonies, impeccable choreography, and dynamic energy. The Temptations' concerts are a celebration of their rich musical legacy, featuring a mix of their greatest hits and fan favorites that continue to resonate with audiences of all generations.

The Temptations' live shows are a testament to their enduring appeal and their ability to create an unforgettable experience for concertgoers. Whether performing in intimate venues or on grand stages, the group's impeccable showmanship and magnetic stage presence have the power to captivate and engage audiences from the moment the curtain rises. Their concerts are an immersive journey through their catalog of timeless classics, showcasing the depth and versatility of their music. Over the years, The Temptations have embraced the opportunities presented by evolving technology and digital platforms to connect with their fans. Social media, streaming platforms, and online communities have provided new avenues for The Temptations to engage with their audience and keep their music alive. Through these digital platforms, fans can access recordings of live performances, behind-the-scenes footage, and interact with the group and fellow fans, fostering a sense of community and connection.

In addition to their own headline tours, The Temptations have also participated in various music festivals, collaborative concerts, and tribute events. These special performances allow them to share the stage with other renowned artists, collaborate with musicians from different genres, and pay homage to their musical influences. These collaborative efforts not only showcase the versatility of The Temptations but also highlight their enduring impact on the music industry as a whole.

The Temptations' commitment to their fans and their passion for performing live is evident in their extensive touring schedule. Despite lineup changes and the passing of time, the group continues to bring their music to audiences around the world, delighting both longtime fans and new listeners.

Their performances are a testament to the enduring power of their music, which transcends generations and resonates with people from all walks of life.

In conclusion, The Temptations' enduring popularity is a testament to their exceptional talent, timeless music, and captivating live performances. Through extensive touring and engagements, the group has maintained a strong connection with their fans and continued to share their music with audiences across the globe. Their concerts are a testament to their enduring legacy, bringing joy and excitement to fans who have been touched by their music for decades. The Temptations' commitment to performing live and their ability to create a memorable experience for their audience ensures that their music will continue to resonate for years to come.

Chapter 46: A Legacy of Music: Iconic Songs and Albums

The Temptations' enduring legacy is defined by their incredible catalog of iconic songs and albums. From their signature harmonies to their soulful performances, the group has created a musical legacy that has stood the test of time. This chapter explores some of The Temptations' most influential songs and albums that have solidified their place in the annals of music history.

One of the most recognizable and beloved songs in The Temptations' repertoire is "My Girl." Released in 1964, the song became an instant classic and remains an anthem of love and devotion. Its infectious melody, heartfelt lyrics, and David Ruffin's lead vocals catapulted the song to the top of the charts and into the hearts of millions of fans worldwide. "My Girl" has become synonymous with The Temptations and continues to be a staple of their live performances.

Another iconic song by The Temptations is "Papa Was a Rollin' Stone." Released in 1972, this powerful and emotionally charged track showcases the group's ability to tackle socially conscious themes. With its haunting instrumentals, deep bass line, and intricate storytelling, "Papa Was a Rollin' Stone" remains a tour de force that delves into the complexities of family dynamics and societal struggles.

The Temptations' albums have also played a significant role in shaping their musical legacy. One of their most influential and critically acclaimed albums is "Cloud Nine" (1969). This groundbreaking release marked a departure from their traditional sound and embraced a fusion of soul, funk, and psychedelic influences. It featured the hit single "Runaway Child, Running Wild" and earned The Temptations their first Grammy Award for Best R&B Performance by a Duo or Group with Vocal. "Cloud Nine" paved the way for their future explorations into new musical territories.

Another notable album is "All Directions" (1972), which further showcased The Temptations' versatility and innovation. The album featured the chart-topping hit "Papa Was a Rollin' Stone" and explored themes of social commentary and introspection. "All Directions" is regarded as a masterpiece, both for its musical arrangements and the group's lyrical depth.

The Temptations' discography is filled with numerous other iconic songs and albums that have left an indelible mark on the music industry. From classics like "Ain't Too Proud to Beg" and "Just My Imagination (Running Away with Me)" to albums like "Gettin' Ready" (1966) and "Masterpiece" (1973), each release showcases the group's incredible talent, harmonies, and ability to evolve with the times.

Furthermore, The Temptations' influence can be heard in the work of countless artists who were inspired by their sound. Their distinctive vocal harmonies, smooth choreography, and the emotional depth of their music have shaped the landscape of R&B and soul music. The Temptations' songs continue to be covered, sampled, and celebrated by musicians across various genres, demonstrating the lasting impact of their music.

In conclusion, The Temptations' legacy of music is characterized by their iconic songs and albums that have become integral parts of popular culture. From the timeless charm of "My Girl" to the profound storytelling of "Papa Was a Rollin' Stone," their music transcends generations and continues to resonate with audiences worldwide. The Temptations' ability to tackle a range of themes, their unmatched vocal harmonies, and their commitment to musical innovation have solidified their place as one of the greatest and most influential groups in the history of popular music. Their songs and albums will forever remain an integral part of the musical landscape, ensuring that The Temptations' legacy lives on for generations to come.

Chapter 47: Celebrating 60 Years of The Temptations

The Temptations' remarkable journey in the music industry has spanned an incredible six decades, leaving an indelible mark on popular music and captivating audiences worldwide. This chapter celebrates the enduring legacy of The Temptations as they reach the milestone of 60 years, reflecting on their incredible achievements, their influence, and the impact they continue to have on the music world.

Throughout their illustrious career, The Temptations have achieved numerous milestones and accolades. They have amassed countless hit songs, earned Grammy Awards, and been inducted into the Rock and Roll Hall of Fame. Their music has topped the charts, and their live performances have enthralled audiences across generations. The group's longevity and continued success are a testament to their exceptional talent, dedication, and ability to evolve with the ever-changing musical landscape.

As The Temptations celebrate 60 years, it is a time to honor their impact and influence on popular culture. Their groundbreaking sound, impeccable harmonies, and dynamic stage presence have inspired countless artists and shaped the landscape of R&B and soul music. The group's ability to seamlessly blend different genres and push artistic boundaries has made them pioneers in their field and paved the way for future generations of musicians.

In addition to their musical contributions, The Temptations have also made a lasting impact through their messages of love, unity, and social consciousness. Songs like "Ball of Confusion" and "War" tackled important social issues of their time, resonating with audiences and providing a platform for meaningful discussions. The Temptations used their platform to advocate for change, and their music became a voice for the voiceless, amplifying the struggles and aspirations of the marginalized.

The Temptations' 60th anniversary is a time to reflect on the collective talent and individual contributions of the group members throughout the years. From the distinctive lead vocals of David Ruffin and the soulful performances of Eddie Kendricks to the smooth harmonies of Melvin Franklin, Paul Williams, and Otis Williams, each member has left an indelible mark on the group's sound and legacy. Their collective artistry and chemistry have solidified The Temptations' status as one of the greatest vocal groups of all time.

As part of the 60th-anniversary celebration, The Temptations embark on a special tour, performing their greatest hits and showcasing the evolution of their music over the years. This tour serves as a testament to their enduring popularity and their ability to captivate audiences with their timeless sound and electrifying performances. Fans both old and new can come together to honor The Temptations' incredible legacy and experience the magic of their live shows.

Furthermore, the 60th anniversary is an opportunity to pay tribute to the loyal fans who have supported The Temptations throughout the years. Their unwavering dedication and love for the group have played a vital role in their continued success. The enduring connection between the fans and The Temptations is a testament to the timeless quality of their music and the profound impact they have had on people's lives.

In conclusion, celebrating 60 years of The Temptations is a testament to their extraordinary talent, longevity, and enduring popularity. From their chart-topping hits to their electrifying live performances, The Temptations have left an indelible mark on the music industry and the hearts of fans around the world. Their contributions to music, their messages of unity and social consciousness, and their unmatched vocal harmonies have cemented their place in music history. As The Temptations continue to inspire and captivate audiences, their 60th anniversary is a time to reflect on their extraordinary journey and to celebrate their lasting legacy.

Chapter 48: The Temptations' Enduring Legacy: Impact on Music and Culture.

The Temptations' enduring legacy extends far beyond their chart-topping hits and mesmerizing performances. Their impact on music and culture is profound, shaping the landscape of popular music and leaving an indelible mark that continues to resonate to this day. This chapter explores the lasting influence of The Temptations and how their contributions have transcended time, genre, and cultural boundaries.

One of the most significant aspects of The Temptations' legacy is their pioneering sound. Their seamless blend of R&B, soul, funk, and pop created a unique and distinctive style that set them apart from their contemporaries. The group's flawless vocal harmonies, led by their exceptional lead singers, created a blueprint for future vocal groups. The Temptations' influence can be heard in the work of countless artists who have followed in their footsteps, from R&B and soul acts to pop, rock, and even hip-hop artists. Their innovative sound continues to inspire and shape the musical landscape to this day.

Beyond their musical contributions, The Temptations played a pivotal role in breaking down racial barriers in the music industry. As one of the first African American groups to achieve mainstream success, they defied stereotypes and challenged societal norms. Their crossover appeal and universal appeal bridged the racial divide, captivating audiences of all backgrounds. The Temptations' success opened doors for other black artists and helped pave the way for greater representation and diversity in the music industry. Moreover, The Temptations' impact on culture extends beyond their music. Their impeccable style, sharp choreography, and polished stage presence set a new standard for performance aesthetics. They were not just singers but true entertainers, captivating audiences with their dynamic and engaging live shows. Their influence can be seen in the artistry and stagecraft of subsequent generations of performers who have drawn inspiration from their captivating performances.

The Temptations' music also served as a mirror to the social and political climate of their time. Songs like "Ball of Confusion," "War," and "Message from a Black Man" addressed pressing issues and gave voice to the concerns of the era. Their socially conscious lyrics and willingness to tackle important topics elevated their music beyond mere entertainment, making them a catalyst for change and a reflection of the times.

The enduring popularity of The Temptations can be attributed to their ability to connect with audiences on a deeply emotional level. Their songs are timeless anthems of love, heartache, and perseverance that resonate with people from all walks of life. Whether it's the romantic ballads that tug at the heartstrings or the powerful, thought-provoking tracks that inspire reflection, The Temptations' music has the power to evoke a range of emotions and touch the human spirit.

Furthermore, The Temptations' legacy is celebrated through their continued influence on popular culture. Their songs are regularly featured in movies, television shows, and commercials, ensuring their music remains a part of the collective consciousness. Tribute acts and revivals keep their music alive on stage, introducing new generations to their timeless sound. The Temptations' iconic choreography, distinctive fashion sense, and smooth harmonies are referenced and emulated by artists across various genres, cementing their status as cultural icons.

In conclusion, The Temptations' enduring legacy lies not only in their chart-topping hits and captivating performances but also in their profound impact on music and culture. Their innovative sound, boundary-breaking success, and socially conscious lyrics have influenced generations of artists and continue to resonate with audiences worldwide. The Temptations' music transcends time, crossing generational divides and cultural boundaries. Their legacy is a testament to the power of music to unite, inspire, and provoke change. As their songs continue to be cherished and celebrated, The Temptations' impact on music and culture remains as strong as ever.

Chapter 49: The Temptations' Continued Relevance: Resonating with New Generations.

The music of The Temptations has stood the test of time, transcending generations and continuing to resonate with audiences around the world. Despite their formation over six decades ago, the group's impact and relevance remain as strong as ever. This chapter explores how The Temptations have maintained their appeal and continue to resonate with new generations of listeners.

One of the key reasons for The Temptations' continued relevance is the timeless quality of their music. Their songs are imbued with universal themes of love, heartbreak, and the human experience, which are relatable to people of all ages. The emotional depth and authenticity of their music allow it to connect with listeners on a profound level, regardless of the era in which they were born. From the soul-stirring melodies of "My Girl" and "Ain't Too Proud to Beg" to the socially conscious messages of "Papa Was a Rollin' Stone" and "Ball of Confusion," The Temptations' catalog boasts a richness and versatility that appeals to music lovers of all backgrounds.

Furthermore, The Temptations' music has found new life through various forms of media and popular culture. Their songs have been prominently featured in films, television shows, and commercials, introducing their music to younger audiences who may not have been familiar with them before. This exposure not only allows new generations to discover and appreciate The Temptations' music but also sparks curiosity and prompts them to explore the group's extensive discography. The enduring popularity of these appearances demonstrates the timeless appeal of The Temptations' sound.

Another factor contributing to The Temptations' continued relevance is the influence they have had on contemporary artists. Many current musicians cite The Temptations as a source of inspiration and influence. From the smooth vocal harmonies to the choreographed stage performances, elements of The Temptations' style can be heard and seen in the work of today's R&B, soul, and pop artists. The group's impact can be seen in the way artists approach their music, stage presence, and overall artistry, ensuring that The Temptations' legacy lives on in the next generation of performers.

Moreover, The Temptations' enduring relevance can be attributed to their ability to adapt to changing musical landscapes while staying true to their core sound. They have collaborated with contemporary artists, explored different genres, and experimented with new sounds, ensuring that their music remains fresh and relevant. This willingness to evolve and embrace new musical directions has allowed The Temptations to maintain a connection with audiences of all ages and remain at the forefront of popular music.

In addition to their musical contributions, The Temptations' commitment to excellence and professionalism has earned them respect and admiration from both fans and industry peers. Their dedication to their craft and their unwavering commitment to delivering exceptional live performances have made them a benchmark for excellence in the music industry. Their iconic choreography, polished stage presence, and captivating energy continue to inspire and captivate audiences, regardless of their age or musical preferences.

Furthermore, The Temptations' continued relevance can be attributed to their enduring presence in live performances. Their timeless hits are regularly performed in concert venues around the world, allowing fans young and old to experience the magic of their music in a live setting. The electrifying energy of a Temptations concert, combined with the nostalgia and excitement generated by their iconic songs, creates an unforgettable experience that keeps audiences coming back for more.

In conclusion, The Temptations' continued relevance is a testament to the enduring power of their music and the universal appeal of their sound. Through their timeless songs, captivating performances, and influence on contemporary artists, The Temptations have solidified their place as one of the most influential and beloved groups in the history of popular music. Their ability to resonate with new generations of listeners ensures that their music will continue to be cherished and celebrated for years to come. The legacy of The Temptations remains as vibrant and relevant today as it was when they first took the stage over six decades ago.

Chapter 50: Appreciating the Timeless Sound: The Temptations' Lasting Influence.

The legacy of The Temptations goes far beyond their chart-topping hits and captivating performances. Their timeless sound and enduring influence have left an indelible mark on the music industry, shaping the landscape of popular music and inspiring generations of artists. This chapter explores the lasting influence of The Temptations and why their music continues to resonate with listeners of all ages.

One of the key factors contributing to The Temptations' lasting influence is their distinctive and timeless sound. Their seamless vocal harmonies, led by their exceptional lead singers, created a signature style that set them apart from their contemporaries. The combination of soulful melodies, rich vocal textures, and impeccable arrangements created a sonic tapestry that captivated audiences and became the hallmark of The Temptations' sound.

The impact of The Temptations' sound can be heard in the work of countless artists across various genres. Their influence is particularly evident in the realms of R&B, soul, and pop music. From the smooth harmonies and intricate vocal arrangements to the infectious rhythms and melodic hooks, elements of The Temptations' sound can be found in the music of artists who have followed in their footsteps. Their innovative approach to vocal harmony and their ability to infuse emotion into every note continue to inspire and shape the musical landscape.

Furthermore, The Temptations' influence extends beyond their musical style. Their artistry and showmanship set a new standard for stage performances. The group's synchronized choreography, polished stage presence, and charismatic energy captivated audiences and established a template for future performers. Their ability to engage and entertain with their live shows continues to inspire and influence artists who strive to create unforgettable experiences for their audiences.

Another aspect of The Temptations' lasting influence is their ability to convey universal themes and emotions through their music. Their songs delve into the depths of love, heartbreak, and the human experience with a rawness and honesty that resonates with listeners of all ages. Whether it's the joyous celebration of love in "My Girl" or the introspective exploration of life's challenges in "Papa Was a Rollin' Stone," The Temptations' lyrics evoke emotions that are timeless and relatable. The enduring relevance of their music lies in its ability to connect on a deeply human level, transcending the boundaries of time and generation.

Moreover, The Temptations' influence on popular culture extends to their fashion sense and visual aesthetics. Their sharp suits, stylish attire, and sophisticated stage presence set them apart as trendsetters and fashion icons. Their impact on fashion and style can still be seen in the choices made by artists today, as they draw inspiration from The Temptations' suave and timeless elegance.

The cultural impact of The Temptations cannot be understated. As one of the first African American groups to achieve mainstream success, they broke down racial barriers and paved the way for greater diversity and representation in the music industry. Their crossover appeal brought people of different backgrounds together, uniting audiences through their shared love of music. The Temptations' success opened doors for future generations of artists, inspiring them to pursue their dreams regardless of their race or background.

In conclusion, The Temptations' lasting influence can be attributed to their timeless sound, exceptional artistry, and ability to connect with listeners on a deep emotional level. Their innovative approach to music, combined with their captivating stage presence and cultural impact, has cemented their place as one of the greatest groups in the history of popular music. As their music continues to be cherished and celebrated by new generations of listeners, The Temptations' influence will undoubtedly endure, ensuring that their legacy lives on for years to come.

Chapter 51: Farewell, But Never Forgotten: The Temptations' Legacy Lives On.

As time marches on, there comes a bittersweet moment when even the most legendary music acts must bid farewell to the stage. The Temptations, after an illustrious career spanning six decades, eventually reached that moment. This chapter pays tribute to the lasting legacy of The Temptations, emphasizing that while their time as a performing group may have come to an end, their influence and impact on music and culture will forever endure.

The Temptations' farewell marked the end of an era, leaving a void in the music industry that will never be filled. The group's final performances were met with a mixture of nostalgia, admiration, and gratitude from fans around the world. It was a chance to celebrate the extraordinary contributions that The Temptations made to the world of music and to honor the lasting imprint they left behind. Though The Temptations as a performing group may have retired, their music continues to captivate and inspire new generations. Their timeless hits, powerful harmonies, and soulful melodies remain as vibrant and relevant today as they were when they were first released. From the joyous and infectious "My Girl" to the thought-provoking "Papa Was a Rollin' Stone," The Temptations' songs continue to resonate with listeners, connecting people across generations and transcending the boundaries of time.

Furthermore, the impact of The Temptations extends beyond their own discography. Their influence can be heard in the work of countless artists who have followed in their footsteps. The group's innovative vocal harmonies, polished stage performances, and signature style have left an indelible mark on the music industry. From R&B and soul to pop and beyond, the echoes of The Temptations can be heard in the music of artists who draw inspiration from their groundbreaking sound.

Moreover, The Temptations' cultural significance and role in breaking down racial barriers cannot be overstated. As one of the first African American groups to achieve mainstream success, they paved the way for greater diversity and representation in the music industry. Their achievements not only shattered glass ceilings but also inspired countless artists, particularly those from marginalized communities, to pursue their dreams and share their unique voices with the world.

The Temptations' enduring legacy is also celebrated through various forms of media and popular culture. Their music continues to be featured in films, television shows, and commercials, ensuring that their songs reach new audiences and remain relevant in the public consciousness. Additionally, the story of The Temptations has been immortalized in biographical works, stage productions, and documentaries, further solidifying their place in the annals of music history.

Beyond their music, The Temptations' legacy is intertwined with the memories and experiences of their dedicated fanbase. Their concerts and live performances created unforgettable moments and lasting connections between the group and their audiences. The energy, charisma, and sheer talent displayed by The Temptations on stage left an indelible impression on those fortunate enough to witness their performances. These cherished memories and the emotional connection forged with fans will forever live on.

In conclusion, while The Temptations' farewell marked the end of an era, their legacy lives on in the hearts and minds of music lovers around the world. Their music continues to inspire, uplift, and transcend generations. The impact of their groundbreaking sound, their cultural significance, and their remarkable achievements will forever be a part of the fabric of music history. The Temptations may have bid farewell to the stage, but their influence and legacy will never be forgotten. They will forever remain an integral part of the musical tapestry, their voices echoing through time, reminding us of the power of soulful harmonies and the enduring spirit of their music.

Resources

Here is a list of resources you can explore for further information on The Temptations and their impact on music and culture:

1. Book: "Temptations" by Otis Williams and Patricia Romanowski - Otis Williams, a founding member of The Temptations, provides an insider's perspective on the group's journey and the challenges they faced.
2. Documentary: "The Temptations" (1998) - This documentary offers a comprehensive

look at the history of The Temptations, featuring interviews with group members, archival footage, and performances.

3. Website: Official Temptations Website - The official website of The Temptations provides information about the group's history, discography, and current news and updates.

4. Article: "The Temptations: The Ultimate Chart History" by Gary Trust (Billboard) - This article provides an overview of The Temptations' chart success and their impact on the Billboard charts.

5. Documentary: "Motown: The Definitive Performances" (2009) - This documentary showcases live performances from Motown artists, including The Temptations, offering a glimpse into their electrifying stage presence.

6. Book: "Dreamgirl & Supreme Faith: My Life as a Supreme" by Mary Wilson - While not solely focused on The Temptations, this memoir by Mary Wilson of The Supremes offers insights into the Motown era and the music industry of the time.

7. Video: The Temptations' performances on The Ed Sullivan Show - Watching their iconic performances on this influential television show provides a glimpse into the group's stage presence and talent.

Please note that availability of resources may vary, so it's recommended to check local libraries, online platforms, and official websites for access to books, documentaries, and articles.

Printed in Great Britain
by Amazon